THE COMPLETE
Bread
BOOK

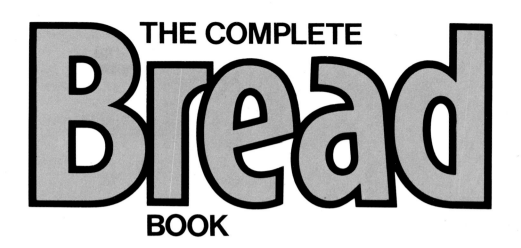

LORNA WALKER
& JOYCE HUGHES

THE COMPLETE
Bread
BOOK

GONDOLA

Hamlyn
London · New York · Sydney · Toronto

Acknowledgements

The authors and publisher would like to thank the following for their co-operation in supplying photographs for this book:

Tower Housewares Limited pages *20–1*
Flour Advisory Bureau *pages 33, 40 and 120*

Photography by Vic Kettle *pages 6–7, 16–17, 24–5, 28–9, 36–7, 44–5, 48–9, 52–3, 56–7, 60–1, 72–3, 76–7, 80–1, 84–5, 88–9, 96–7, 100–1, 108–9, 116–17, 124–5 140–1 and 168–9*
Photography by John Lee *title page and pages 64–5, 92–3, 132–3, 136–7, 144–5, 148–9, 152–3, 156–7, 160–1, 164–5 and 174–5*

Pictor International *endpapers*

Spectrum Colour Library *pages 11 and 13*

Cover photograph by James Jackson
Line drawings by Gay John Galsworthy

Pictured on previous pages *Harvest Sheaf (see page 66) and Irish Potato Bread (page 117)*
Pictures on pages 6–7 *Assortment of breads including Cinnamon Orange Swirl (see page 63), Croissants au Beurre (page 103), Gala Tea Ring (page 51) and Ring Doughnuts (page 46)*

First published 1977 by The Hamlyn Publishing Group Limited
First published 1983 as a Hamlyn Gondola Book by
The Hamlyn Publishing Group Limited
London · New York · Sydney · Toronto
Astronaut House, Feltham, Middlesex, England

ISBN 0 600 32355 2

Printed in Hong Kong

Contents

Introduction

Do you kick the cat, count worry beads or hurl objects at your nearest and dearest when the pressure and tension of life becomes overwhelming? Be productive, not destructive . . . take up breadmaking and punch your aggressions out on the dough!

Apart from its therapeutic effect, breadmaking offers a variety of delicious home-baked breads and buns, which can be made not only to personal choice, but more important, most economically. Admittedly the crusty white loaves and rolls freshly baked by small bakers are hard to beat but when it comes to variety and wholesomeness the home-baked breads win hands down. The smell of freshly baked bread does wonders for the family appetite, tantalises the neighbours, and is rewarding to the cook because her time and effort (if effort it may be considered) is so much appreciated. In fact, once you establish a routine, breadmaking becomes effortless – ask any breadmaker.

One of the objects of our writing this book is to give confidence to the new breadmaker by collecting all the facts for her to have at her fingertips. In addition the established breadmaker will find a host of new recipes and ideas to add to her repertoire of well tried favourites.

We are most grateful to the various embassies and to the Beadle at Baker's Hall for their help whilst researching this book – and we would also like to thank friends, particularly Betty Jakens for introducing us to each other, and colleagues, especially those at the Flour Advisory Bureau, who over the years helped us build up our knowledge and experience. Finally we would like to thank our husbands and sons who have eaten their way through a large variety of breads and given their 'honest' opinion whilst we were trying and testing all the recipes for the book.

Lorna. Walker

Joyce Hughes.

Useful Facts and Figures

NOTES ON METRICATION

In this book quantities are given in metric and Imperial measures. Exact conversion from Imperial to metric measures does not usually give very convenient working quantities and so the metric measures have been rounded off into more useful units of grams or millilitres. The tables below show the recommended equivalents.

Solid and dry ingredients

Imperial	Approx. g to nearest whole figure	Recommended equivalent
½ oz	14 g	15 g
1	28	25
1½	42	40
2	57	50
3	85	75
4 (¼ lb)	113	100
5	142	150
6	170	175
7	198	200
8 (½ lb)	227	225
9	255	250
10	283	275
11	312	300
12 (¾ lb)	340	350
13	368	375
14	397	400
15	425	425
16 (1 lb)	454	450
2 lb	907	1 kilogram

Liquid and fluid ingredients

Imperial	Approx. ml to nearest whole figure	Recommended equivalent
2 fl oz (3 tablespoons)	57 ml	50 ml
4 (6 tablespoons)	113	100
5 (¼ pint)	142	150
6	170	175
7	198	200
8	227	225
9	255	250
10 (½ pint)	283	300
11	312	325
12	340	350
13	368	375
14	397	400
15 (¾ pint)	425	450
18	510	500 (0·5 litre)
20 (1 pint)	567	600
1¼ pints	709	750 (0·75 litre)
1½ pints	851	900
1¾ pints	992	1 litre

When converting quantities larger than those given, first add the appropriate figures in the centre column, then adjust to the nearest unit of 25. As a general guide, 1 kg (1000 g) equals 2·2 lb or about 2 lb 3 oz; 1 litre (1000 ml) equals 1·76 pints or almost exactly 1¾ pints. For quantities of 1¾ pints and over the recipes call for litres and fractions of a litre. For some bread recipes a more exact conversion has been used in order to preserve the balance between the ingredients.

Spoon measures are level unless otherwise indicated. Three teaspoons equal one tablespoon.

Can sizes in the UK at present are marked with the exact (usually to the nearest whole figure) metric equivalent of the Imperial weight of the contents, so we have followed this practice when giving can sizes.

Loaf tins used in these recipes are small (450-g/1-lb), which have an approximate liquid capacity of 900 ml/1½ pints, or large (1-kg/2-lb), which have a 1·75-litre/3-pint liquid capacity.

OVEN TEMPERATURES
The table below gives recommended equivalents.

	°C.	°F.	Gas Mark
Very cool	110	225	¼
	120	250	½
Cool	140	275	1
	150	300	2
Moderate	160	325	3
	180	350	4
Moderately hot	190	375	5
	200	400	6
Hot	220	425	7
	230	450	8
Very hot	240	475	9

Follow only one set of figures for any particular recipe, as they are not interchangeable.

NOTES FOR AUSTRALIAN USERS
Ingredients in this book are given in metric and Imperial measures. In Australia the standard 250-ml measuring cup is used in conjunction with the Imperial pint of 20 fluid ounces. However, for the purposes of this book it is most important to remember that the Australian tablespoon differs from both the American tablespoon and from that used in these recipes. The British standard tablespoon holds 17·7 millilitres and the Australian 20 millilitres. A teaspoon holds approximately 5 millilitres in both systems. The table below gives a quick comparison.

British	Australian
1 teaspoon	1 teaspoon
1 tablespoon	1 tablespoon
2 tablespoons	2 tablespoons
3½ tablespoons	3 tablespoons
4 tablespoons	3½ tablespoons

9

Chapter 1

A Short History of Bread

For at least 8000 years man has been making bread – a very long time, going back some 6000 years before Christ was born to the New Stone Age. Stone was then used to make tools to hoe the ground, to cut down the crop and then to separate the grain. Crushed between stones, the grain gave a crude flour which was mixed to a dough with water, shaped to a round, flat cake and then cooked on a large flat stone over a fire. As you may imagine, the result – a rather hard bread – was very different from the light textured loaf we know today.

Even with the passing of some considerable time, and with it increased knowledge of the cultivation of wheat and the grinding of flour, bread did not improve greatly; it is interesting to note that although the Egyptians of the XI Dynasty (2050 BC) had well preserved teeth they were, alas, worn down by continual chewing, perhaps of bread that was coarse, hard and gritty! An example of the bread eaten then, a loaf over 4000 years old, can be seen today in the Egyptian gallery of the British Museum.

However, bread did improve quite dramatically somewhat later with the discovery of how to make it rise: the story goes that a forgetful young Egyptian left some uncooked dough sitting for some time before he remembered it, and during this time the dough fermented. This caused the dough to rise when it was made into loaves so that on baking the loaves, our young Egyptian baker found he had produced the first light textured risen bread.

The Egyptians became so expert at growing wheat in quantity that they produced more than they needed for their own needs and began to export it. The Greeks, who bought the Egyptian wheat, developed such variety and skill as breadmakers that they became the master bakers of their time. When they conquered the Greeks, the Romans – ever-willing pupils – learned a lot from the skill of the Greek bakers and started a college for bakers to improve and teach this knowledge. It is said that by the year 100 BC there were 258 bakers' shops in Rome. The eruption of the volcano Vesuvius at Pompeii in 79 AD produced a lava flow which transfixed life and allows us to see today something of what it was like to be living at that time. Not only were there bakers' shops where loaves of bread were stamped with the makers' initials but also public ovens where people could bake their own bread. The more wealthy residents, of course, had their own ovens.

Like us the Romans graded their grain. The finer and whiter bread was considered the best and was reserved for the nobility, wholemeal was eaten by the mass of people and the rough (Cibarus) was for slaves, convicts and the Navy.

When Cassius arrived in Britain with the conquering Romans it is said he was so disgusted with the home-produced bread that he had his sent all the way from Rome . . . stale bread from Rome being preferable to the fresh British variety! The British had a lot to learn, and apart from the many sophisticated improvements (like central heating) the Romans made they did a lot to upgrade the quality of bread. They improved agricultural methods and imported hard wheat, which could not be grown in Britain. This is much better for bread-making because it absorbs more liquid than the British soft wheats; this extra water works on the wheat protein to give a more elastic dough and therefore a lighter loaf. The Romans also introduced the circular mill-stone and the technique of turning it by the use of water. After the Romans left, Britain deteriorated in many ways, and little can be said for the progress of bread during the Dark Ages when the veneer of Roman civilisation wore down to nothing with the repeated onslaughts of invasions from Scandinavia and Europe.

With the Norman invasion, however, matters did improve a little: in 1191 records first tell of the Norman windmill – a useful way to mill flour for those not living near running water. The Normans drank a great deal of beer and yeasted breads were again popular. The bread of the time was large, flat and round, not well risen because once again soft home-grown wheat was used. Nevertheless the bread was useful due to its

French baker's trade sign,
late 19th century

plate shape, as it was frequently used for just that purpose. These breads were called trenchers and it is from this that we get the expression 'to be a good trencherman', which was the description applied to a man who could knock back his dinner and his trencher as well!

For breadmaking flour a sack of corn would be taken to the miller for grinding; as payment he was allowed to keep a proportion of the corn. This system made for easy fraud, and some millers fell under suspicion of taking a few sly handfuls extra. The millers were not the only ones: bread was frequently taken to the local baker for baking in his oven and if the loaf came back smaller than expected the baker would be accused of stealing a piece of the dough before baking. Perhaps there was some justification for this mistrust – the case is recorded of an artful baker who cut a hole in his kneading board and kept a boy underneath to take off pieces of dough right under the customer's eye! Both to protect the public from these unscrupulous traders and to guard their own good name the bakers formed themselves into a brotherhood or guild first known as The Fraternity of St. Clement of the Mistery of Bakers. One of the prime duties of the Guild officers was to prevent dishonesty among their members by means of spot inspections of sizes, weights and prices of bread.

The officers also ensured bakers were maintaining the standards laid down by the Guild for bakehouses and the living and working conditions of apprentices. Apprenticeships lasted for seven years, as the bakers liked to keep the 'Mistery' of baking to themselves, thus making it difficult for outsiders to move in on their trade. An interesting condition affecting apprentices was that they were not allowed to be served salmon more than twice a week. Salmon at that time was a common fish in the Thames.

Four times a year, a special court was held to read formally the rules of the baking trade and to bring bakers who had transgressed these rules to rather unpleasant justice. If guilt were proven, often a cheating baker was punished by being hauled through the streets for a very rough ride on a hurdle, with his loaves tied round his neck. His angry customers took good advantage of this by hurling not only abuse at him but bad eggs and squashed tomatoes as well!

As the Guild grew in size and importance the bakers decided their position justified becoming a chartered company. They obtained a charter from Henry VII in 1486 and also purchased a hall for their meetings. Every year on the Sunday after St. Clement's Day (St. Clement being their patron saint) they elected a Master and four Wardens. In their coat of arms an anchor was incorporated to symbolise St. Clement's rather nasty death (he was thrown overboard from a boat with an anchor tied round his neck!). A bakers' hall still stands on the site where the first hall was built in 1506.

Because of the unpleasant sentences that could be applied to bakers selling underweight loaves, they protected themselves by baking an extra 'make-weight' loaf to every dozen . . . hence the expression 'a baker's dozen'.

During the 17th century with increased prosperity bread improved once more. There was plenty of wheat and rye to make bread, which was often of mixed grains. In 1602 it was written: 'The English husband-men eat barley and rye brown bread as abiding longer in the stomach and not so soon digest with their labour: but citizens and gentlemen eat most pure white bread.'

Thus white bread continued to be a luxury enjoyed only by the rich. An observer noted in 1750: 'English-men of all classes became so dainty as to insist on refined wheat bread that had previously been regarded as a luxury for the rich.'

In the 19th century, although wheat was plentiful, Parliament put such heavy duties on imported wheat that the price of bread soared to as much as two shillings and sixpence per loaf, when some wages were only three shillings a week. People revolted against these duties as embodied in the Corn Laws, and in 1846 after a series of riots the laws were repealed.

The 20th century is the age of mechanisation, mass production, electrification and automation. More women go out to work and less baking is done at home. For many, the factory loaf provides a convenient an-swer to today's needs as it is wrapped and sliced ready to use. However, although one would not really wish to bring back the so-called 'good old days', it would be satisfying to bring back the good things associated with times gone by such as the slower pace of life, fresh flavoursome food and home baking. Breadmaking is one of the basics and also one of the most rewarding aspects of home baking. Do not be inhibited by the aura surrounding it: once mastered, breadmaking is simple. There is something inherently satisfying about preparing a loaf of bread with 8000 years of tradition behind it.

Bread Freezing Chart

Item to be Frozen	Does it Freeze?	How to Wrap	Storage Time	Thawing	Comment
Fresh Yeast	Yes – but note comment	Divide into usable 25-g/1-oz cubes & wrap each tightly in cling film then pack into a polythene box.	Up to 6 months	Grate while frozen for immediate use or thaw at room temperature for 30 minutes (it will not be as solid as fresh yeast).	When using frozen yeast to get best results use 50% more than recipe calls for.
Dried Yeast	Yes	Place packets in polythene bag or freeze cans as they are.		Use from freezer.	
Raw Bread Dough (white or brown flour)	Yes – but note comment	After mixing and kneading dough place it (in quantities it is likely to be cooked in) in oiled polythene bags – seal and freeze.	Up to 6 months. If the dough is enriched with fat or eggs, or if it has been given a first rise, for best results do not keep longer than 4 months.	Loosen bag to allow space for dough to rise – then leave at room temperature for 5–6 hours.	Dough is now ready to be left in bag to rise then shaped & risen again before baking. As yeast seems to lose some of its effect when frozen, increase basic proportion of yeast by 50%, i.e. 25 g/1 oz to 40 g/1½ oz.
Part-Baked Rolls	Yes – very well	Cook rolls for 5 minutes in a hot oven, then for a further 10 minutes in a cool oven. Cool, then place flat on tray in freezer until just frozen, then store in a sealed polythene bag.	Up to 4 months	Preheat moderately hot oven and bake frozen rolls on a baking tray for 20 minutes.	This is one of the best ways to prepare rolls for the freezer.
Bread (soft thin-crusted large loaves)	Yes – well	Wrap in polythene bags and seal.	Up to 6 months	Leave wrapped at room temperature for about 4 hours.	It may be wrapped in foil and heated through in a moderately hot oven for about 45 minutes then left until cold; but leaving at room temperature is best.
Bread (crisp-crusted loaves)	Yes – but see comment	Wrap in foil.	Up to 1 week	Place foil parcel in a moderately hot oven for about 30 minutes (or until loaf feels soft) then open up parcel and cook for a further 10 minutes to crisp up crust.	After about 1 week the crust begins to flake off.
French or Vienna Loaves	Not really satisfactory; this type of bread is always best eaten fresh.	Wrap in foil or polythene bags.	Up to 3 days	Thaw at room temperature then crisp crust in a hot oven.	If this bread is thawed in a hot oven the crust becomes over-crisp before the centre is soft.
Soft Rolls	Yes – well	In polythene bags.	Up to 4 months	Thaw packed at room temperature or wrapped in foil in a hot oven for 15 minutes.	
Croissants	Yes – well	Arrange flat on foil trays then cover with foil.	Up to 3 months	Leave in pack for about 1½ hours, then place it in a hot oven for 5–10 minutes before unwrapping, although the frozen pack may be placed in a moderate oven for about 15 minutes.	The uncooked dough may also be frozen before it is shaped.

Item to be Frozen	Does it Freeze?	How to Wrap	Storage Time	Thawing	Comment
Danish Pastries	Yes – well	If iced place pastries unwrapped in freezer, then wrap. If not iced pack in polythene bags.	Up to 6 months	Uncover icing otherwise thaw wrapped at room temperature for about 1½ hours, then place in a hot oven for about 5 minutes.	
Rich Yeast Teabreads	Yes – very well	Wrap in polythene. If any are decorated with whipped cream or soaked in sauces (e.g. babas) freeze uncovered then wrap.	Up to 3 months	Items which had to be frozen before packing should be unpacked before thawing otherwise thaw packed.	
Pizza	Yes – well	Prepare pizza until it is ready to bake then freeze flat until solid before wrapping.	Up to 3 months	Unwrap, place frozen pizza in a hot oven and bake for 35 minutes from cold or until cooked through.	The pizza may also be frozen when cooked (it will store up to 2 months and have to be reheated from frozen for about 20 minutes in a hot oven) but the freshly baked pizza gives the best results for less time overall.
Flat Soft Breads	Yes	Pack together in polythene bags.	Up to 3 months	Thaw wrapped at room temperature for about 2 hours.	Some of the Indian breads are best warmed through (after thawing) on a hot griddle or frying pan.
Flat Crisp Breads	Yes – some	In polythene bags.	Up to 1 month	Unwrap and thaw at room temperature.	Flatbröds freeze well but the crust of crisp thin yeasted breads flakes off quite quickly.
Soda & Scone Breads	Yes	In polythene bags.	Up to 6 months	Leave wrapped and thaw at room temperature for about 2 hours. Place in a hot oven for about 5 minutes to crisp up.	
Richer Teabreads (without yeast)	Yes – well	In foil or polythene bags.	Up to 6 months	Thaw wrapped for 2–3 hours at room temperature.	
Flavoured Butter Breads (to be served hot from the oven)	Yes – see comment	Cut a French or Vienna loaf in thick slices (not cutting through the base), spread both sides of each slice fairly thickly with butter mashed with crushed garlic or herbs, allowing to each loaf 50 g/2 oz butter, 1 clove garlic or 1 tablespoon finely chopped fresh herbs. Wrap loaf in foil.	Up to 1 week	Place wrapped in a moderately hot oven for about 30 minutes. Unwrap parcel for a further 5 minutes so crust can crisp up.	These flavoured breads are so popular they are a useful standby to have in the freezer to serve with soups, casseroles or supper dishes. If you make your own Vienna-type bread do not cook it long enough for the crust to crisp; then when used for flavoured butter breads it will keep much longer in the freezer without the crust flaking off.
Breadcrumbs, Fresh or Buttered	Yes – well	In polythene bags.	Up to 3 months (1 month if buttered)	Can be used frozen.	Frozen crumbs are very useful to have in store for all kinds of sweet or savoury dishes.
Croûtons & Fried Bread Shapes	Yes	Pack the cold fried bread shapes in a polythene bag.	Up to 1 month	Bake from frozen, flat on a baking sheet in a moderately hot oven for 5 minutes.	Frozen croûtons are ideal to keep ready to sprinkle over soups and thus save a last-minute job. The fried shapes make good bases for party canapés or hot savoury snacks.
Snack Sandwiches	Yes – see comment	Wrap each individually in polythene bags.	Up to 2 months	They may be thawed at room temperature or, if to be served hot, cooked from frozen.	Most foods can be used for fillings except salad stuffs or egg.

Chapter 2

Bread for Beginners

Breadmaking is surprisingly simple and good results are certain if you understand the ingredients used and follow the simple rules. It is also economical since only small quantities of the more expensive ingredients such as sugar and fat are used.

The main ingredients in breadmaking are flour, yeast, salt and liquid. Other ingredients may be added e.g. sugar, fat, eggs, soya flour, dried fruits and malt to give the wide variety of breads which we know. There is also a group of breads risen with chemical raising agents rather than yeast, known as 'soda' or 'tea' breads.

FLOUR

The term 'flour' when used in recipes refers to wheat flour unless otherwise indicated:

The choice of flour for breadmaking with yeast is important. For best results a strong plain flour or bread flour which has a high protein content (10–15%) should be used. The protein in the flour forms a substance called *gluten* when water is added and develops into an elastic-like solid when kneaded. Strong or high protein flours absorb more liquid and quickly develop with kneading into firm elastic doughs giving a larger volume and lighter texture when baked into bread than soft flours. A soft flour with a low protein content (7–10%) absorbs less liquid and gives a smaller volume and closer texture.

Flours are not always specifically labelled strong or soft, but the information or recipe on the bag will probably give a good indication of its type. If you are not sure ask your supplier or contact the miller direct.

The American all-purpose flour also known as 'general purpose' is a strong flour and will give similar results to the British strong or bread flour.

Colours of Flour White flours usually contain 70–72% of the cleaned wheat grain. The bran and germ which give wholewheat or brown flours their colour are removed when white flour is milled (although sometimes a little remains).

Brown and wheatmeal flours usually contain 80–90% of the cleaned wheat grain after milling, i.e. some of the bran and germ are removed.

Wholewheat or wholemeal flours contain the whole of the cleaned wheat grain after milling. It can be coarse, medium or finely ground. Stone-ground flour is a wholewheat flour produced by grinding the wheat grain between stones instead of steel rollers.

Wholewheat or brown flours give variety in colour and flavour to bread. Because they contain all, or a high proportion of, the bran and germ, which have a softening effect on the protein in the flour, bread baked from these flours will have a limited rise and closer texture than those made with white flour.

In breadmaking where yeast is used as the raising agent, plain flour should be used unless otherwise stated.

Self-raising Flours These are usually soft or all-purpose household flours, i.e. medium strong, to which raising ingredients have been added by the miller. The usual raising ingredients are sodium bicarbonate and acid calcium phosphate, which yield carbon dioxide in the form of a gas during baking.

Self-raising flour may be used in non-yeasted tea-breads although some cooks prefer to use plain flour to which they can add a varying quantity of raising agent to suit the particular recipe and method.

Proprietary Flours and Meals In addition to the ordinary white, brown and wholewheat flours a few proprietary flours are available for making speciality breads. The majority of these mixes, which contain varying amounts of wheat germ, bran, whole wheat grains, soya flour, malt flour and in some cases other cereals such as rye and barley, are only readily available to the baker and occasionally as packaged mixes to the housewife through the grocer.

Nutritional Value of Wheat Flour and Bread Flour, and hence bread, supplies energy, protein, calcium, iron and vitamins of the B group.

White and brown flours vary slightly in nutritional value according to their composition; however, as there is a policy of enrichment with iron, thiamine (vitamin B_1), niacin and calcium, for flours of less than 80% extraction rate, and since we eat a wide variety of food, there is little significant difference in the nutritional values of flours and hence breads whether white or brown.

Government surveys show that bread plays an important part in the average national diet in the UK. It provides over one-fifth of a person's daily thiamine intake; nearly one-sixth of the daily protein, iron, calcium, niacin and energy value. This means, of course, that the importance of including bread, whether homemade or bought, in one's diet should never be underestimated.

Non-wheat Flours used in Breadmaking These include rye flour, rice flour, soya flour, cornmeal and oatmeal. Rye flour is available as light, when some of the branny outer layers are removed, and dark, similar to American rye graham flour which is a coarse textured flour ground from the entire rye grain. Since rye flour does not form much gluten it produces baked products which are small in volume and close in texture. However, it is often mixed with other flours in breadmaking and is used on the Continent for making 'black' bread.

Rice flour is a flour milled from white rice and is finer than ground rice. It contains no gluten-forming proteins and may therefore be used in gluten-free diets. It produces baked products of small volume and close texture.

Soya flour is prepared by grinding treated soya beans whose hulls have been removed. It has a distinct flavour and is occasionally added to wheat flour to enhance the nutritional value of baked products.

Cornmeal is a type of flour milled from corn (maize). It is more readily available in America, where it is frequently used in bread recipes. However, it can sometimes be found in the international food departments of some large stores in the UK.

Oatmeal is produced by grinding cleaned oats. It is obtainable in coarse, medium or fine meal textures, and was once used extensively throughout the UK, when oats were grown in large quantities. However, they have been replaced by wheat and barley in many areas and as a result oatmeal is now used less.

Storage of Flour Flour can lose or gain moisture, thus affecting its storage life. The best way to store flour is in its bag on a cool dry airy shelf. If the kitchen is rather damp or steamy, put the bag in an airtight container.

Under these conditions plain flour keeps well for 4–6 months; self-raising flour for 2–3 months; wholewheat or wheatmeal flours for up to 2 months.

YEAST

Yeast is a traditional raising agent, known since earliest times by its ability to break down food materials containing starch and sugar into alcohol and carbon dioxide gas.

Yeast is living matter composed of tiny cells which we cannot see without the aid of a microscope. These cells live all around us – in the air, in the ground and on the fruits and leaves of many plants.

There exists a great variety of yeasts in nature and some are specially suited for breadmaking. These selected strains of yeast are isolated, specially bred and cultivated scientifically under controlled conditions, and then are produced in huge quantities and sold as baker's compressed yeast (fresh yeast). This yeast, in addition to being sold in blocks as fresh yeast, may also be dried so that the cells will remain alive through many months of storage in a cool place. This is called active dried baking yeast.

In breadmaking it is the gas, carbon dioxide, given off during the rising and proving periods which is important. The gas forms bubbles in the dough which cause it to rise and give the finished (baked) bread its familiar porous structure which makes it light. The small amount of alcohol produced is driven off by the heat of the oven, and the by-products that are formed during the working of the yeast give the bread its special flavour. Yeast is a source of all the B vitamins, although some of these are destroyed by heat during baking.

Fresh Yeast should be creamy in colour, cool to touch and crumble when broken. It is most usually available from bakers' or health food shops.

To keep it fresh, store in a cold place in a screw top jar, plastic lidded container or a polythene bag. It will keep 4–5 days in a cold larder or 1–2 weeks in a refrigerator. Fresh yeast may be frozen for up to 6 months, but it is advisable to first divide it into portions most likely to be used, i.e. 15 g/½ oz, 25 g/1 oz and then wrap individually in foil or polythene film and store in a plastic box or polythene bag in the freezer. In this way the correct amount can be taken from the freezer, defrosted and used immediately.

Active Dried Baking Yeast is composed of dry granules similar in colour to fresh yeast. It is packed in small packets or airtight cans and is available from many grocers, chemists and health food stores.

It is convenient to use for domestic baking as it can be kept for several months in a tightly lidded can in a cool place and be available for use when required. If there is much air space in the can it will not keep as well, so change to a smaller container for longer storage periods. When in doubt as to the activity of the yeast after a long storage period, a quick check may be made by reconstituting a small quantity as recommended; if after 10 minutes the yeast granules have dissolved and the liquid has a frothy head then it should have sufficient activity to make satisfactory bread. If little activity has occurred after 10 minutes it would be advisable to discard the yeast to avoid disappointing results.

Dried yeast is more concentrated than fresh yeast, therefore one requires approximately one-third to one-half the quantity of fresh yeast. 25 g/1 oz fresh yeast is equivalent to 15 g/½ oz or 3 teaspoons of dried yeast.

Different Methods of Adding Yeast to Flour There are three traditional methods of adding yeast to flour and the method chosen usually depends on the type of dough being prepared.

1 *The dissolved yeast method* is suitable for all yeast recipes.

Fresh yeast Blend with some or all of the liquid and add to the flour and remaining ingredients to make a dough. Cold liquid may be used but warm (38°–43°C./100°–110°F.) gives a quicker rise.

Dried yeast Dissolve a teaspoon of sugar or honey in some or all of the warm liquid (38°–43°C./100°–110°F.). Sprinkle in the dried yeast and leave in a warm place for 10 minutes or until frothy, then add to the remaining ingredients to make a dough.

2 *The batter method* is particularly useful for preparing rich yeast mixtures containing fairly high proportions of fat, sugar and egg. In such doughs the growth of yeast is retarded but this may be overcome by first forming a batter of:

one-third of the flour in the recipe
all the yeast – fresh or dried
all the liquid – warm (38°–43°C./100°–110°F.)
some of the sugar (1 teaspoon)

No salt should be added at this stage since this slows down the yeast. Leave the covered batter to stand in a warm place until it froths up like a sponge (about 20 minutes with fresh yeast, 30 minutes with dried yeast). Then add the rest of the flour, salt and other ingredients such as fat, eggs, or fruit and mix to a firm dough.

3 *The rubbing-in method* is the easiest method but is only suitable for fresh yeast and for soft doughs and quick breads.

Rub the yeast into the flour (it is not necessary to break it up completely), add the liquid and make a soft dough. Beat well with the hand, a wooden spoon or fork to distribute the yeast evenly.

Note Yeast is killed at high temperatures (over 60°C./140°F.) so the mixing, rising and proving stages must all be completed below this temperature. When the dough is placed in the hot oven, the heat kills the yeast, no further carbon dioxide is given off and the rising ceases. At cool temperatures the action of yeast is retarded but the yeast is not killed (see paragraph on rising).

THE OTHER INGREDIENTS

Salt gives flavour to yeasted goods and prevents the yeast from fermenting too quickly. Too much salt kills the yeast, while the omission of salt results in a dough which becomes sticky rather than elastic after rising and which produces a loaf of poor volume and shape.

Sugar is a food for yeast. When sugar is added to a recipe and fresh yeast is being used it is inadvisable to

Overleaf *Varied shapes for Plain White (see page 30) and Wholewheat breads (page 31) and French Bread (page 102)*

cream the yeast with all the sugar, since a high concentration of sugar tends to kill some of the yeast cells.

Sugar has a softening action on the gluten and, therefore, rich doughs containing considerable amounts of sugar have a closer texture than those with little or no sugar. Sugar also helps the crust to brown and adds flavour. Brown sugar, honey or molasses may be used as a substitute for white sugar.

Fat, which may be butter, margarine or lard, enriches doughs, improves the softness and colour of the crumb and delays staling. Cooking oil may be used, but it does not produce the same improvement in the colour of the crumb and may even give a greyish colour.

Liquid may be water, milk, a mixture of both or fruit juice. The quantity varies depending on the flour and the recipe.

300 ml / ½ pint liquid to 450 g / 1 lb strong flour is a useful guide. Soft flour will take less. It is better to add all the liquid at once, and then extra flour may be added if the dough is too sticky for easy handling. It is difficult to add more liquid to a dough once formed if it is too dry.

Milk adds extra food value and improves the keeping quality and crust colour. Fruit juices, such as orange and tomato juices, strengthen the gluten and give baked goods a good volume as well as unusual colour and flavour. Many of the recipes in this book refer to 'warm liquid', which means liquid at a temperature of 38°–43°C. / 100°–110°F. This can be obtained by mixing 2 parts cold liquid with 1 part boiling liquid, i.e. 300 ml / ½ pint cold water and 150 ml / ¼ pint boiling water.

Eggs added to doughs make richer breads with an increased food value. They also improve the structure and add colour.

Dried fruits and malt are added to doughs to make richer and more varied breads. It is advisable to warm dried fruit before adding it to the dough, since this precaution eliminates the slowing down of the fermentation or rising which occurs when cold fruit is added to the dough. Malt has a softening effect on gluten and, therefore, malt breads tend to have a close, sticky texture.

Raising agents other than yeast may be either baking powder or a mixture of bicarbonate of soda and an acid ingredient which in the presence of moisture and heat e.g. during baking, liberates carbon dioxide to give a rise to the batter or dough.

Vitamin C (ascorbic acid) is a fairly recent ingredient in certain types of breadmaking, namely the 'short-time' breads. It is not added to enhance the nutritional value of bread since it is all lost during baking; however, the addition of a small amount of vitamin C reduces, and almost cuts out, the first rising period thereby reducing the total time of breadmaking considerably.

Vitamin C tablets are obtainable from chemists in 25-mg, 50-mg and 100-mg sizes.

THE DIFFERENT STAGES OF BREADMAKING AND THEIR IMPORTANCE

Mixing This can be carried out by hand or in a mixer using a dough hook.

By hand Add all the liquid to the dry ingredients and mix with the hand, a wooden spoon or fork until a scone-like dough, which leaves the bowl clean, is formed, adding more flour if the dough is too sticky to handle.

With a mixer Read manufacturer's instructions regarding the quantity of dough which the machine using the dough hook can accommodate without causing undue strain on the motor. In several of the more popular domestic mixers this is based on 675 g / 1½ lb flour.

Place all the liquid in the bowl first and then add the dry ingredients. Using the dough hook, turn to the lowest speed and mix for 1– 2 minutes to form a dough.

Kneading All yeast doughs must be kneaded after mixing. Kneading develops and strengthens the gluten in the dough which can be seen when the rough inextensible dough becomes smooth and elastic. This is necessary for good rise and even crumb texture. As with mixing it can be carried out by hand or in a mixer. Kneading by hand is extremely relaxing. It is also worth noting that children enjoy and are good at kneading dough!

By hand This should be done on a flat surface (table, counter top or board) using little or no flour. To begin, form the dough into a ball. First fold the dough towards you, then using the heel of your hand push the dough away with a rolling motion. Turn the dough one quarter turn around and repeat kneading, developing a rocking rhythm. If the dough becomes sticky, sprinkle the work surface and your hands with a little flour. Continue for about 10 minutes until the dough is smooth and elastic.

With a mixer Place the dough in the bowl and using the dough hook turn the mixer on to second speed for 2–3 minutes until the dough is smooth and elastic.

Rising All yeast doughs must be risen *at least once* before baking to allow time for the yeast to work. The oven temperature during baking will quickly kill the yeast and, therefore, the dough must be fully risen before it goes into the oven. (A small increase in volume will take place in the oven, known as 'oven-spring', but this cannot replace the rising outside the oven.) A risen dough should be at least double its original volume. If the dough has overrisen and collapsed, remove from container, knead well and rise again.

Doughs must be covered during rising to prevent formation of a surface skin and loss of heat. Unshaped doughs can be left in the mixing bowl and covered with a large polythene bag; they can also be placed directly inside a large lightly oiled polythene bag tied at the top to allow plenty of room for rising, or a lightly greased plastic storage jar, saucepan or casserole with lid. Shaped doughs in tins or on baking sheets should be placed inside large lightly oiled polythene bags tied loosely.

To oil polythene bags place a few drops of cooking oil inside the bag and rub the sides of the bag together to spread the oil.

Rising times vary with temperature and the type of dough and can be chosen to suit your convenience.

A warm place (not too hot or the yeast will be killed) gives a quick rise and a refrigerator a slow rise. Rich doughs take longer to rise than plain doughs. When time allows, a slow rise gives better results, because it controls yeast growth. For a plain dough the approximate rising times are as follows:

45–60 minutes in a warm place (not above 38°C./100°F.)

1½–2 hours at room temperature (18°–21°C./63°–70°F.)

8 hours in a cold larder

12–18 hours in a refrigerator (4°C./40°F. or under)

Overnight rising A cold larder or refrigerator has a useful place in yeast cookery. A dough may be mixed the night before it is required, using cold ingredients, and left covered in a cold larder or refrigerator overnight. The dough is then knocked-back, shaped, risen and baked the following day. This is particularly useful for rich soft doughs which are slow to rise and are difficult to shape when warm. Shaped doughs may also be refrigerated overnight but they must be returned to room temperature and the rising must be completed, if necessary, before baking.

Doughs may also be frozen (see pages 14–15 for freezing information).

Shaping To shape, the risen dough must first be 'knocked-back', i.e. flattened firmly with the knuckles and kneaded for 1–2 minutes to make the dough firm again. This knocks out the air bubbles and ensures an even rise in the shaped doughs. Avoid using too much flour on the work surface at this stage, since this will spoil the colour of the crust.

The basic shaping for tin loaves, cobs and dinner rolls are given here and the more unusual shapes are given under individual recipe instructions.

Tin loaf Cut off and weigh 500 g/1 lb 2 oz dough for a small (450-g/1-lb) loaf tin or 1 kg/2 lb 4 oz dough for a large (1-kg/2-lb) loaf tin.

Flatten the dough using your hands to form an oblong the same length as the tin and approximately three times as wide. Roll up the dough like a Swiss roll and turn so that the seam is underneath when placed in tin. Smooth over the top, tuck under ends to give a slightly domed appearance and drop into a greased tin. Best results are obtained if the tins are warmed before greasing and filling with dough.

Cob Cut off and weigh 350 g/12 oz dough for a small cob or 675 g/1 lb 8 oz dough for a large cob. Shape into a round and place on a greased baking tray.

Dinner rolls and buns Cut off and weigh 50-g/2-oz pieces of dough. Knead each piece of dough for a short time and shape into a smooth ball. This is best done on an unfloured surface with a little flour on the palm of the hand. Place palm of hand on dough and press down hard, then roll the dough round under palm of hand, slowly easing up the hand. Place on a greased baking tray.

Proving (Second Rising) The shaped dough must be risen again, or proved, and this is done by placing the tins or baking sheets containing the dough inside large lightly oiled polythene bags, tied loosely at the top or with open end tucked under tin, allowing plenty of space for the dough to rise. The dough must double in size or in the case of tin loaves be risen about 2·5 cm/1 inch above the top of the tins. This proving or rising time also depends on the temperature at which it takes place but is usually a little shorter than the first rising period.

Finishes Loaves and rolls may be left plain, dusted with flour, or brushed with salt water, milk, fat or egg wash before baking. Cracked wheat or poppy seeds are often sprinkled over the top of brown and white breads respectively. Cracked wheat can be obtained from health food shops or prepared from whole wheat grains in a blender. Poppy seeds can be obtained from some specialist food shops. Fruit and sweet breads may be brushed with clear honey or sugar glaze after baking.

Egg wash Beat together 1 egg, 1 teaspoon sugar and 1 tablespoon water.

Sugar glaze Dissolve 50 g/2 oz sugar in 4 tablespoons water or milk over a low heat. Bring to the boil and boil rapidly for 2 minutes.

Baking The cover e.g. polythene bag used during proving must be removed before baking.

Loaves are baked in the centre of a hot oven and rolls nearer the top. Specific oven temperatures and times are given in each recipe as it would be impractical to give them here.

The test for baked loaves and rolls is that the crust of white loaves and rolls should be golden brown and that of brown loaves and rolls well formed and browned. A cooked loaf shrinks slightly from the sides of its tin and when turned out of the tin should sound hollow when tapped on the bottom with the knuckles. For a crisper crust, tin loaves may be switched from their tins to a baking sheet for the last 5 minutes of baking.

Short-Time Method of Breadmaking This is a fairly modern method which enables bread to be made in approximately 1¾–2 hours. This method requires the addition of a small amount of vitamin C which reduces the first rising period to almost nothing, thereby reducing the total time considerably.

The first rising for short-time doughs is reduced to 5 minutes' resting for plain doughs and 10 minutes' resting for enriched doughs. The second rising or proving after shaping will take 45–50 minutes at room temperature (21°C./70°F.) and 40 minutes in a warm place (32°C./90°F.).

A slight readjustment of the basic recipe for bread is necessary when using this method, in that the quantity of yeast is increased and a little sugar added to those recipes without sugar. Fresh yeast is recommended since dried yeast causes the dough to take 1 hour longer to rise with this method, which defeats the object of the method. The vitamin C is dissolved in the yeast liquid.

SOME USEFUL HINTS FOR SUCCESS IN BREADMAKING

1 Choose the right flour – a strong plain flour known as bread flour.
2 Add the yeast correctly according to the method chosen.
3 Add all the liquid at once.
4 Knead the dough thoroughly, about 10 minutes by hand, 2–3 minutes using a dough hook and mixer.
5 Cover the dough when rising or proving to prevent a surface skin forming.
6 Make sure the dough is properly risen by following the instructions for rising and proving carefully.
7 Bake at the correct temperature given in the recipe.

COMMON FAULTS AND HOW TO AVOID THEM

Fault	Possible cause	How to avoid
1. Poor volume and close texture.	1. Flour too soft. 2. Too much salt. 3. Under-proving (rising). 4. Oven too cool.	1. Use a strong flour. 2. Measure the salt carefully. 3. Make sure the dough is risen to double its original volume. 4. Check the oven temperature with an oven thermometer or call in appropriate fuel board representative.
2. Uneven texture and holes.	1. Too much yeast. 2. Insufficient kneading and knocking-back. 3. Over-proving (rising).	1. Measure or weigh the yeast carefully. 2. Make sure kneading is carried out correctly. 3. Allow a shorter proving time and if you suspect that a dough is over-proved, i.e. it is beginning to collapse, knock-back, reshape and prove again.
3. Strong yeasty flavour.	1. Too much yeast. 2. Dried yeast not reconstituted properly. 3. Fresh yeast creamed with sugar.	1. Measure or weigh the yeast carefully. 2. Make sure that the dried yeast is fully reconstituted, i.e. no dry granules remain undissolved. 3. Do not cream fresh yeast with too much sugar.
4. 'Flying top' (crust pulled away unevenly from top of loaf).	1. Flour too soft. 2. Under-proving (rising).	1. Use a strong flour. 2. Allow a longer proving (rising) time.

A SIMPLE RECIPE FOR BEGINNERS

Wheatmeal Bread

Makes 2 small loaves or 12 rolls

This recipe is for a small quantity of dough, 675 g / 1½ lb, since it is advisable to begin with a fairly small quantity and when success is achieved then larger quantities may easily be tackled. A short kneading period of only 2 minutes is allowed in this recipe since the baked loaf should have a fairly close texture (because half the flour used is brown). A longer kneading period will not make a substantial difference to the texture of the bread and, therefore, is felt to be unnecessary for the beginner.

For those beginners who wish to produce bread quickly, but who are not too concerned about the lightness of the loaf, the first rising period may be omitted and the dough shaped immediately after mixing and kneading, and then left to prove.

METRIC / IMPERIAL
225 g / 8 oz strong white flour
225 g / 8 oz wheatmeal flour
2 teaspoons salt
15 g / ½ oz lard
2 teaspoons castor sugar
15 g / ½ oz fresh yeast or 2 teaspoons dried yeast
300 ml / ½ pint water

Mix the flours and salt in a bowl and rub in the lard. *To make dough with fresh yeast*, mix the sugar into the flour. Blend the yeast in the water until it has dissolved, then add to the flour all at once. Mix to a scone-like dough which leaves the bowl clean, adding a little more white or brown flour if too sticky to handle. *To make dough with dried yeast*, mix 1 teaspoon sugar into the flour. Dissolve the other teaspoon of sugar in warm water and sprinkle in the dried yeast. Leave in a warm place for 10 minutes, or until frothy. Add to the flour all at once. Mix to a scone-like dough as with fresh yeast.

Knead the dough for about 2 minutes until smooth.

*Place inside an oiled polythene bag and leave to rise until doubled in size.

Remove the polythene bag, knock-back and knead for 1–2 minutes.*

To make loaves, divide the dough into 2 pieces and shape each piece to fit a well greased 450-g / 1-lb loaf tin. To make rolls, divide the dough into 12 pieces and form each piece into a roll. Place well apart on greased baking trays. Brush the tops with water and sprinkle with cracked wheat or crushed wheat flakes, if liked.

Put the tins or baking trays in a large lightly oiled polythene bag and leave to prove until dough has doubled in size.

Remove from the polythene bag. Bake the loaves in the centre of a hot oven (230°C., 450°F., Gas Mark 8) for approximately 30 minutes; bake the rolls on second shelf from top of a hot oven for approximately 15 minutes. Turn out and cool on a wire rack.

Note From * to * in the method may be omitted. This is obviously quicker, but the texture of the baked loaves and rolls will be coarser.

Chapter 3

Basic Bread Recipes with Yeast

All the recipes in this chapter can be prepared by a standard method or by the short-time method. The standard method varies according to the type of dough, i.e. plain or rich, but always includes two rising periods, the second being referred to as 'proving'. The texture and volume of the baked loaves or rolls are improved by two rising periods; however, an equally satisfactory texture and volume can be obtained by the addition of vitamin C to the yeast liquid in the short-time method when the first rising period is reduced.

If you do not have a vitamin C tablet, and do not mind a loaf or rolls with a coarser texture and slightly smaller volume, then omit the first rising period in the standard method and shape the dough immediately after mixing and kneading. However, when time is available (remember overnight rising), it is worth including the first rising period in the standard method to obtain delicious, light loaves and rolls with an even texture and good volume.

The recipes are all based on 675-g/1½-lb or 450-g/ 1-lb flour weights, since these are suitable for most mixers with a dough hook. The quantities may be doubled if wished, but larger quantities should be mixed by hand as they are too heavy for most mixers.

Plain White Bread

Standard Method

Yields approximately 1·1 kg/2 lb dough
Makes 1 large or 2 small loaves or 18 rolls

METRIC/IMPERIAL
15 g/½ oz fresh yeast or 2 teaspoons dried yeast
1 teaspoon castor sugar
400 ml/¾ pint warm water or milk or milk and water
675 g/1½ lb strong white flour
2 teaspoons salt
15 g/½ oz lard or margarine

Prepare the yeast liquid: blend the fresh yeast in the warm liquid until it has dissolved or dissolve 1 teaspoon sugar in the warm liquid, then sprinkle in the dried yeast. Leave in a warm place for 10 minutes or until dissolved and frothy.

Mix the flour and salt together and rub in the fat. Add the yeast liquid to the dry ingredients and mix to form a firm dough, adding extra flour if it is too sticky to handle.

Turn the dough onto a lightly floured surface and knead until smooth and elastic and no longer sticky. It will take about 10 minutes by hand or 2–3 minutes using a mixer and dough hook.

Shape the dough into a ball, place inside a large oiled polythene bag and leave to rise until it is doubled in size. Remove from the polythene bag, knock-back and knead until the dough is firm, about 2 minutes. Shape into loaves and/or rolls. The loaves or rolls may be left plain, lightly dusted with flour, or brushed with milk or egg wash before baking. Cover and prove.

Bake the loaves in the centre of a hot oven (230°C.,

Previous pages Plain White Bread, Wholewheat Plait and Rolls (see page 31)

450°F., Gas Mark 8) for approximately 40 minutes for large (1-kg/2-lb) tin loaves; 30–35 minutes for small (450-g/1-lb) tin loaves, or until the loaves shrink slightly from the sides of the tin and the crust is deep golden brown. Bake large cob loaves for 35–40 minutes; small cob loaves for approximately 30 minutes; dinner rolls for 15–20 minutes.

Alternative shapes
Farmhouse tin loaf Use all of the dough. Grease and well flour a large (1-kg/2-lb) loaf tin. Flatten the dough with the hands to form an oblong the same length as the tin and approximately three times as wide. Fold the dough into three and drop it into the tin with the join underneath and the ends just folded under to give the top a domed appearance. Dust the surface with flour. Cover and prove. When proved, before baking, make a slit with a sharp knife along the centre of the top parallel to the long sides of the tin. Bake as for a large tin loaf.

Cottage loaf Use all the dough to make one large cottage loaf or divide in half to make two smaller loaves. Cut off one-third and knead both pieces into rounds. Place the larger round on a greased baking sheet. Brush the top with water and place the smaller round on top. Push two floured fingers down the centre of both rounds to fix them firmly together. Cover and prove. Bake in the centre of a hot oven (230°C., 450°F., Gas Mark 8) for approximately 40 minutes for a large loaf and 30–35 minutes for small loaves.

Crown loaf Cut off and weigh 350 g/12 oz risen dough. Divide into 6 equal pieces. Roll each piece into a smooth ball. Place 5 dough balls in a ring in a greased 15-cm/6-inch sandwich tin or flan ring and place the sixth in the centre. Brush with egg wash and sprinkle with poppy seeds, if liked. Cover and prove. Bake in the centre of a hot oven (230°C., 450°F., Gas Mark 8) for 25–30 minutes.

Bloomer Cut off and weigh 350 g/12 oz risen dough. Shape into a fat roll approximately 15 cm/6 inches long. Place on a greased baking tray and make diagonal slashes with a sharp knife along the top. Cover and prove. Bake in the centre of a hot oven (230°C., 450°F., Gas Mark 8) for about 25 minutes.

Bridge and finger rolls Cut off and weigh 25-g/1-oz pieces of risen dough for small bridge rolls; 50-g/2-oz pieces for medium rolls or 75-g/3-oz pieces for large rolls. Knead each piece of dough and roll into a thin sausage shape, slightly tapering off at the ends, about 7 cm/3 inches long for the 25-g/1-oz pieces, about 10 cm/4 inches long for the 50-g/2-oz pieces and about 13 cm/5 inches long for the 75-g/3-oz pieces. It is easier to use both hands when rolling the dough: spread the fingers over the dough and roll them backwards and forwards until the dough reaches the desired length. Place rolls well apart on a greased baking tray. Brush with milk or egg wash. Cover and prove. Bake in the centre of a hot oven (230°C., 450°F., Gas Mark 8) for 15–20 minutes.

Cloverleaf rolls Cut off and weigh 50-g/2-oz pieces of the risen dough. Divide each piece equally into 3 parts and shape into 3 small balls. Place on a greased baking tray in the shape of a cloverleaf, pressing lightly together, or alternatively place the 3 small balls together in a greased bun tin. Brush with egg wash. Bake in the centre of a hot oven (230°C., 450°F., Gas Mark 8) for 15–20 minutes.

Twists and knots Cut off and weigh 50-g/2-oz pieces of risen dough. Roll each piece into long thin strands using both hands. Tie into knots or twist into figures of eight or coils. Place on a greased baking tray. Brush with milk or egg wash. Cover and prove. Bake in the centre of a hot oven (230°C., 450°F., Gas Mark 8) for 15–20 minutes.

Soft dinner rolls Cut off and weigh 50-g/2-oz pieces of risen dough. Shape into rolls. Place 2 cm/¾ inch apart on a greased and floured baking tray or tin. Brush with melted butter or margarine and lightly dust with flour. Cover and prove. Bake in the centre of a hot oven (230°C., 450°F., Gas Mark 8) for 15–20 minutes. (The rolls will join together when baking.)

Plain White Bread

Short-Time Method

Yields approximately 1·1 kg /2½ lb dough
Makes 1 large or 2 small loaves or 18 rolls

METRIC/IMPERIAL
25 g/1 oz fresh yeast
275 ml/½ pint cold water
125 ml/¼ pint boiling water
25-mg vitamin C tablet
675 g/1½ lb strong white flour
2 teaspoons salt
2 teaspoons sugar
15 g/½ oz lard or margarine

Prepare the yeast liquid: blend the fresh yeast in the warm water obtained by mixing the cold water with the boiling water. Add the vitamin C tablet and stir until dissolved. Put the flour, salt and sugar in a large bowl and rub in the fat. Add the yeast liquid to the dry ingredients and mix to form a firm dough, adding extra flour if it is too sticky to handle.

Turn the dough onto a lightly floured surface and knead until smooth and elastic. It will take about 10 minutes by hand or 3 minutes with a mixer and dough hook.

Shape the dough into a ball and place inside a large oiled polythene bag and leave to rest for 5 minutes. Remove the polythene bag and divide into the required amounts. For a large loaf baked in a large (1-kg/2-lb) loaf tin, use all the dough. For two small loaves baked in two small (450-g/1-lb) loaf tins divide the dough in half. For rolls divide the dough into 50-g/2-oz pieces. Shape as required.

Place the tins or baking trays inside large lightly oiled polythene bags and leave loaves to rise for about 50 minutes at room temperature or about 40 minutes in a warm place; rolls for about 30 minutes at room temperature or 25 minutes in a warm place.

Remove the polythene bags and bake loaves and rolls at the same temperature and times as given under Plain White Bread (Standard Method).

Wholewheat Bread

Standard Method

Yields approximately 1·1 kg /2½ lb dough
Makes 1 large or 2 small loaves or 18 rolls

METRIC/IMPERIAL
25 g/1 oz fresh yeast or 3 teaspoons dried yeast
400 ml/¾ pint warm water
1 tablespoon soft brown sugar
675 g/1½ lb wholewheat flour
2 teaspoons salt
15 g/½ oz butter, vegetable fat or oil

Prepare the yeast liquid: blend the fresh yeast in the water until dissolved, or dissolve 1 teaspoon of the measured sugar in the warm water and sprinkle in the dried yeast. Leave in a warm place for 10 minutes or until dissolved and frothy.

Mix together the flour and salt. Rub in the fat and then mix in the sugar. Add the yeast liquid to the dry ingredients and mix to form a firm dough, adding extra flour if it is too sticky to handle.

Turn the dough onto a lightly floured surface and knead thoroughly until smooth and elastic. It will take 5–10 minutes by hand or 2–3 minutes with a mixer and dough hook.

Shape the dough into a ball and place inside a large oiled polythene bag and leave to rise until doubled in size. Remove the polythene bag, knock-back and knead until the dough is firm, about 2 minutes.

Shape into loaves and/or rolls using all the dough for a large (1-kg/2-lb) loaf tin or large cob, half the dough for a small (450-g/1-lb) loaf tin or small cob and 50-g/2-oz pieces of the dough for rolls. The loaves or rolls may be left plain, lightly dusted with wholewheat flour, or brushed with salted water or milk and sprinkled with cracked or crushed wheat. Cover and prove.

Bake the loaves in the centre of a hot oven (230°C., 450°F., Gas Mark 8) for approximately 40 minutes for large loaves and 30–35 minutes for small loaves. Turn the loaves out of the tins and tap the bases with the knuckles – they will sound hollow if ready. Bake dinner rolls for 15–20 minutes. Turn out onto a wire rack.

Alternative shapes
Tin rolls loaf Use half the dough and divide into 4 pieces. Roll each piece into a round ball as described for forming dinner rolls. Place the rolls side by side in a well greased small loaf tin. Brush with salted water and sprinkle with cracked or crushed wheat. Cover and prove. Bake in the centre of a hot oven (230°C., 450°F., Gas Mark 8) for 30–35 minutes.

Plait Use half the dough and divide into 3 pieces. Roll each piece into a 35-cm/14-inch length, slightly tapering off at the ends. Join the 3 strands together at one end, plait the strands evenly and pinch the ends together to join. Place on a greased baking tray, brush with salted water and sprinkle with cracked or crushed wheat if liked. Cover and prove. Bake in the centre of a hot oven (230°C., 450°F., Gas Mark 8) for 25–30 minutes.

Coburg Use half the dough and shape into a round cob. Place on a greased baking tray and cut a fairly deep cross in the top of the loaf. Brush with milk and sprinkle with wholewheat flour. Cover and prove. Bake in the centre of a hot oven (230°C., 450°F., Gas Mark 8) for 30 minutes.

Pot loaves Use one-third of the dough to make a pot loaf baked in a 10–12-cm/4–5-inch earthenware flower pot or similar volume earthenware pot. Prepare the clean pot by greasing well and baking it empty in the hot oven three or four times to prevent the loaf sticking. (Once this initial preparation has been carried out, it is only necessary to grease well before use.) Shape the dough to fit the pot. Brush the top with salted water and sprinkle with cracked or crushed wheat. Cover and prove. Bake in the centre of a hot oven (230°C., 450°F., Gas Mark 8) for 30 minutes.

Wholewheat Bread

Short-Time Method

Yields approximately 1·1 kg/2½ lb dough
Makes 1 large or 2 small loaves or 18 rolls

METRIC/IMPERIAL
25 g/1 oz fresh yeast
300 ml/½ pint cold water
150 ml/¼ pint boiling water
25-mg vitamin C tablet
675 g/1½ lb wholewheat flour
1 tablespoon salt
1 tablespoon brown sugar
15 g/½ oz lard

Follow instructions for Plain White Bread (Short-Time Method).

Shape as for Wholewheat Bread (Standard Method).

To prove, place the tins or baking trays inside large lightly oiled polythene bags and leave the loaves to rise for about 50 minutes at room temperature or about 40 minutes in a warm place and the rolls for about 30 minutes at room temperature or 25 minutes in a warm place.

Remove the polythene bags and bake the loaves and/or rolls at the same temperature and times as given under Wholewheat Bread (Standard Method).

Rich Milk Bread

Standard Method

Yields approximately 850 g/1 lb 14 oz dough
Makes 1 large or 2 small plaits or twists or 12–14 fancy rolls
The standard method for this bread is the sponge batter method which is especially good for recipes rich in fat and/or sugar.

METRIC/IMPERIAL
450 g/1 lb strong white flour
1 teaspoon castor sugar
15 g/½ oz fresh yeast or 1½ teaspoons dried yeast
250 ml/8 fl oz warm milk
1 teaspoon salt
50 g/2 oz butter or margarine
1 standard egg

Prepare the yeast batter: mix together 100 g/4 oz flour, the sugar, fresh or dried yeast and the warm milk in a large bowl. Cover and set aside until bubbly, about 20 minutes in a warm place, longer in a cool one.

Mix the remaining flour with the salt and rub in the fat. Beat the egg, add to the yeast batter with the dry ingredients, and mix well to give a soft dough, adding extra flour if the dough is too sticky to handle.

Turn the dough onto a lightly floured surface and knead until smooth and elastic. It will take about 10 minutes by hand or 2–3 minutes with a mixer and dough hook. Shape the dough into a ball and place inside a large oiled polythene bag and leave to rise until doubled in size. Turn the risen dough onto a lightly floured surface, knock-back and knead until the dough is firm, about 2 minutes. Shape into plaits and/or rolls, using 50-g/2-oz pieces of risen dough, as required.

Cover and prove. Brush with egg wash. Sprinkle with poppy seeds if wished. Bake in the centre of a moderately hot oven (190°C., 375°F., Gas Mark 5) until the plait is a rich brown and sounds hollow when the base is tapped, allowing about 40–45 minutes for a large twist or plait or 35–40 minutes for a small twist or plait.

Alternative shapes
Twist Use all of the dough for a large twist or half for a small twist. Divide the dough in half and roll each

Crown Loaf (see page 30), Plaits (page 31), Coburg (page 32) and Twists and Knots (page 31)

piece out into a strand 35 cm/14 inches long. Cross the 2 strands at their centres. Take the 2 ends of the bottom strand and cross them over in the centre. Repeat this with the 2 ends of the other strand. Cross each strand alternately, building the twist vertically until all the dough is used up. Finally pinch the ends together and lay the twist on its side on a greased baking tray. Cover and prove. Remove cover, brush with egg wash and sprinkle with poppy seeds, if wished.

Crown loaf Use 350 g/12 oz risen dough. Cover and prove. Brush with egg wash and sprinkle with poppy seeds, if wished. Bake in the centre of a moderately hot oven (190°C., 375°F., Gas Mark 5) for about 35 minutes or until the loaf sounds hollow when the base is tapped.

Cloverleaf rolls Bake towards the top of a moderately hot oven (190°C., 375°F., Gas Mark 5) for 15–20 minutes.

Twists and knots Bake towards the top of a moderately hot oven (190°C., 375°F., Gas Mark 5) for 20–25 minutes.

Star rolls Shape each piece of dough as for a round dinner roll. Place the rolls well apart on a greased baking tray. Cover and prove. Remove the cover and make 5 snips with scissors in each roll from the edge of the roll almost to the centre to form a star shape. Bake towards the top of a moderately hot oven (190°C., 375°F., Gas Mark 5) for 20–25 minutes. Brush the hot rolls with thin honey after baking.

Parkerhouse rolls Shape each piece of dough into a roll. Cover with oiled polythene and leave to rest for 10 minutes. Flatten each roll into a circle, using either a rolling pin or the palm of your hand. Brush the dough with melted margarine or butter. Make a depression just off the centre of the circle with the handle of a wooden spoon or knife, fold over and press down edge. Place on a greased baking tray. Cover and prove. Bake towards the top of a moderately hot oven (190°C., 375°F., Gas Mark 5) for 20–25 minutes.

Crescents Use 350 g/12 oz risen dough. Knead into a ball, then cover with oiled polythene and leave to rest for 10 minutes. Roll out into a circle, 5 mm/¼ inch thick and brush with melted butter or margarine. Cut into 8 wedge-shaped pieces. Roll up, beginning at the outer edge, and curve into crescent shapes. Place on a greased baking tray, making sure the point (or end) is on the underside. Cover and prove. Brush with egg wash and bake towards the top of a moderately hot oven (190°C., 375°F., Gas Mark 5) for 20–25 minutes.

Rich Milk Bread

Short-Time Method

Yields approximately 850 g/1 lb 14 oz dough
Makes 1 large or 2 small plaits or twists or 12–14 fancy rolls

METRIC/IMPERIAL
25 g/1 oz fresh yeast
250 ml/8 fl oz warm milk
25-mg vitamin C tablet
450 g/1 lb strong white flour
1 teaspoon salt
1 teaspoon castor sugar
50 g/2 oz butter or margarine
1 standard egg

Prepare the yeast liquid: blend the fresh yeast in the warm milk. Add the vitamin C tablet and stir until dissolved. Put the flour, salt and sugar in a large bowl and rub in the fat. Add the yeast liquid and the lightly beaten egg to the dry ingredients and mix to form a firm dough, adding extra flour if it is too sticky to handle.

Turn the dough onto a lightly floured surface and knead until smooth and elastic. It will take about 10 minutes by hand or 3 minutes with a mixer and dough hook.

Shape the dough into a ball and place inside a large oiled polythene bag or replace in a greased mixing bowl. Cover and leave to rest for 10 minutes. Turn out the dough and divide into the required amounts. Shape as described under Rich Milk Bread (Standard Method). Place the baking trays inside large lightly oiled polythene bags and leave the plaits or twists to rise for about 50–60 minutes at room temperature or 40–45 minutes in a warm place; leave the rolls for about 30 minutes at room temperature or 25 minutes in a warm place.

Remove polythene bags and bake the plaits, twists or rolls at the same temperature and times as given under Rich Milk Bread (Standard Method).

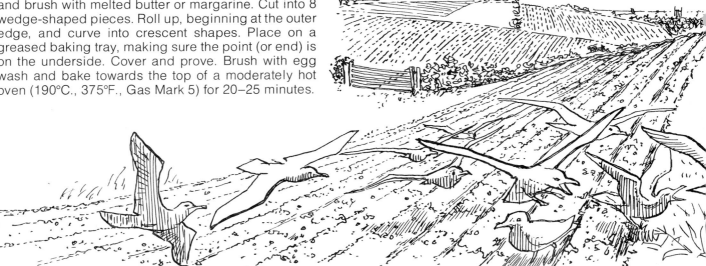

Sweet Bread

Short-Time Method

Yields 850 g / 1 lb 14 oz dough
Makes 2 loaves or 16 buns

METRIC / IMPERIAL
25 g / 1 oz fresh yeast
100 ml / 4 fl oz cold milk
75 ml / 3 fl oz boiling water
25-mg vitamin C tablet
450 g / 1 lb strong white flour
1 teaspoon salt
50 g / 2 oz butter or margarine
50 g / 2 oz castor sugar
1 standard egg

Follow the instructions for making Rich Milk Bread (Short-Time Method). Shape the dough as described under Sweet Bread (Standard Method).

Place the baking trays inside large lightly oiled polythene bags and leave the loaves to rise for about 50–60 minutes at room temperature or 40–45 minutes in a warm place, or the buns for about 30 minutes at room temperature or 25 minutes in a warm place.

Bake and finish the loaves and buns at the same temperature and times as for Sweet Bread (Standard Method).

Sweet Bread

Standard Method

Yields 850 g / 1 lb 14 oz dough
Makes 2 loaves or 16 buns

METRIC / IMPERIAL
450 g / 1 lb strong white flour
1 teaspoon castor sugar
25 g / 1 oz fresh yeast or 3 teaspoons dried yeast
100 ml / 4 fl oz cold milk
75 ml / 3 fl oz boiling water
1 teaspoon salt
50 g / 2 oz butter or margarine
50 g / 2 oz castor sugar
1 standard egg

Prepare the yeast batter: put 100 g / 4 oz flour, 1 teaspoon castor sugar, and the fresh or dried yeast in a large bowl. Combine the cold milk and boiling water and mix well. Cover and set aside until bubbly, about 20 minutes in a warm place, longer in a cool one.

Mix the remaining flour with the salt, then rub in the fat and stir in the remaining sugar. Beat the egg and add to the yeast batter with the dry ingredients and mix well to give a soft dough, adding extra flour if the dough is too sticky to handle.

Turn the dough onto a lightly floured surface and knead until smooth and elastic. It will take about 10 minutes by hand or 2–3 minutes with a mixer and dough hook. Shape the dough into a ball and place inside a large oiled polythene bag and leave to rise until doubled in size.

(A cooler dough is easier to shape, but refrigerated dough must be left at room temperature for 1 hour before shaping.)

Turn the risen dough onto a lightly floured surface, knock-back and knead until the dough is firm, for about 2 minutes. Shape into loaves and / or buns as required. Cover and prove. Remove cover and bake loaves in the centre and buns just above the centre of a moderately hot oven (190°C., 375°F., Gas Mark 5) allowing 15–20 minutes for buns and about 35–40 minutes for a large loaf or twist or 30–35 minutes for a small loaf or twist, until the loaf is a rich brown and sounds hollow when the base is tapped. Brush the warm loaves or buns with a sugar glaze and cool on a wire tray.

Chapter 4
Variations on Basic Doughs

Yeast bread recipes and doughs are extremely versatile and allow us to prepare a large variety of breads from a few basic recipes. Variety may be obtained by the addition of ingredients to a basic dough at the mixing stage, by adding ingredients to the risen or rested doughs or simply by forming different shapes.

It is sometimes necessary to adjust the basic recipe and when this is the case e.g. Tomato Bread, the adjusted basic recipe is given. However, it is often more useful to make a selection of breads from a risen dough, or, in the case of doughs prepared by the short-time method, the rested dough. Risen or rested dough may be used to make a large variety of fancy breads, rolls and buns.

In this chapter recipes are given which will allow you to make a selection of baked breads from one dough e.g. from one quantity of plain white bread dough you can make a small tin loaf, a currant loaf and 6 cheese rolls, or from one quantity of wholewheat bread dough you can make a small cob, 4 dinner rolls and 9 savoury rolled buns. Make up the basic dough recipes in quantities sufficient to cover your selection.

Care should be taken when mixing additional ingredients into a dough to ensure that they are all well mixed in. Some doughs may be rather sticky but in these cases a note to this effect is made; it is not advisable to use additional flour.

VARIATIONS ON PLAIN WHITE BREAD

Standard Method (see page 30) or Short-Time Method (see page 31)

Malt Bread

Makes 3 small loaves

This is a soft sweet bread which because of the softening effect of malt on the gluten does not have a big rise and is risen only once; however, it is necessary to increase the amount of yeast in the basic recipe to obtain even this smaller rise. Malt bread keeps well and is delicious served buttered.

METRIC/IMPERIAL
25 g/1 oz fresh yeast or 3 teaspoons dried yeast
1 teaspoon castor sugar
350 ml/12 fl oz warm water
175 g/6 oz malt extract
50 g/2 oz black treacle
25 g/1 oz butter or margarine
675 g/1½ lb strong white flour
15 g/½ oz salt
100 g/4 oz sultanas (optional)

Prepare the yeast liquid as for Plain White Bread (see page 30). Gently heat the malt extract, treacle and fat until the fat has melted. Cool. Add the yeast liquid and cooled malt mixture to the dry ingredients and mix to form a soft dough.

(This dough will be too sticky to knead. Beat well either by hand or using a wooden spoon or mixer for 2–3 minutes to develop the gluten.)

Spoon into three well greased small (450-g/1-lb) loaf tins. Cover and prove for at least 2 hours in a warm place, or longer in a cool place, until the mixture reaches 1 cm/½ inch below the top of the tins. Remove covers and bake in the centre of a moderately hot oven (200°C., 400°F., Gas Mark 6) for 35–40 minutes. Remove from the tins and brush the tops with a sugar glaze while still hot.

Tomato Bread

Makes 2 small loaves or 24 rolls

Part of the liquid in this recipe is replaced by tomato purée which gives this bread an unusual colour and flavour. It is ideal for serving with salads or made into bridge rolls for parties.

METRIC/IMPERIAL
15 g/½ oz fresh yeast or 1½ teaspoons dried yeast
1 teaspoon castor sugar
300 ml/½ pint warm water
150 g/5 oz tomato purée
675 g/1½ lb strong white flour
15 g/½ oz salt
½ teaspoon onion or garlic salt
1 teaspoon paprika pepper
15 g/½ oz lard or margarine

Prepare the yeast liquid as for Plain White Bread (see page 30) using only 150 ml/¼ pint of the warm water. Blend the tomato purée with the remaining water. Add the yeast liquid and tomato liquid to the dry ingredients and follow the method for Plain White Bread.

Shape into loaves or rolls as required. Brush with egg wash. Cover and prove. Bake the loaves in the centre of a hot oven (220°C., 425°F., Gas Mark 7) for 30–35 minutes and the rolls towards the top of the oven for 15–20 minutes. Turn out and cool.

Onion Bread

Makes 2 small loaves or 3 batons or 24 rolls

A delicious savoury bread obtained by adding onion soup mix to the flour. Ideal for serving with cheese or salad dishes.

METRIC/IMPERIAL
15 g/½ oz fresh yeast or 1½ teaspoons dried yeast
1 teaspoon castor sugar
450 ml/16 fl oz warm water
675 g/1½ lb strong white flour
40 g/1½ oz dry onion soup mix
15 g/½ oz salt
25 g/1 oz lard or margarine

Follow the method for making Plain White Bread (see page 30), adding the dry onion soup mix to the flour. Shape into loaves, rolls or batons. To make a baton, cut off and use one-third (400 g/14 oz) of the dough. Roll the dough out to a sausage shape about 25 cm/10 inches long, tapering at the ends. Make diagonal slashes at 2·5-cm/1-inch intervals along the top with a sharp knife. Place on a greased baking tray. Brush all loaves, rolls or batons with egg wash. Cover and prove.

Bake in the centre of a hot oven (220°C., 425°F., Gas Mark 7) for about 30–35 minutes for tin loaves and towards the top of the oven for 15–20 minutes for rolls and about 25 minutes for batons. Turn out and cool.

Cheese Bread

Makes 1 small loaf or 8 rolls

METRIC/IMPERIAL
400 g/14 oz risen plain white dough
75 g/3 oz Cheddar cheese, grated
½ teaspoon dry mustard
¼ teaspoon pepper

Reserve a little cheese for sprinkling over the top of the loaf or rolls. Add the remainder with the mustard and pepper to the dough. Squeeze and knead into the dough by hand until the cheese is evenly mixed through the dough.

Shape to fit a well greased small (450-g/1-lb) loaf tin or divide into 50-g/2-oz pieces and shape into rolls. Brush with milk or egg wash. Cover and prove.

Bake the loaf in the centre of a hot oven (220°C., 425°F., Gas Mark 7) for 30–35 minutes and rolls towards the top of the oven for 15–20 minutes. Sprinkle reserved cheese on top of loaf or rolls 5 minutes before the end of the cooking time. Turn out and cool on a wire rack.

Note Wholewheat or wheatmeal risen dough can be substituted (see page 31).

Variation
Cheese plait Use the full amount of basic dough, i.e. 1·1 kg/2½ lb, and twice the amount of cheese. Divide two-thirds of the dough into 3 equal pieces. Roll each piece into a strand approximately 30 cm/12 inches long. Join the 3 strands together at one end, plait the strands and pinch together remaining ends. Roll the remaining one-third of dough into 2 strands about 25 cm/10 inches long. Join at one end and shape as for a large twist (see page 32). Lay it down the centre of the plait. Place on a greased baking tray. Cover and prove. Brush egg wash over the surface of the plait. Sprinkle with poppy seeds if liked. Bake in the centre of a hot oven (220°C., 425°F., Gas Mark 7) for about 35–40 minutes. Turn out and cool.

Cheese and Onion Bread

Makes 1 small loaf or 8 rolls

METRIC/IMPERIAL
400 g/14 oz risen plain white dough
15 g/½ oz margarine or oil
25 g/1 oz onion, finely chopped
50 g/2 oz Cheddar cheese, grated

Melt the margarine or heat the oil gently and fry the onion slowly until soft and transparent but not at all coloured. Add most of the cheese and the onion to the dough and squeeze and knead into the dough by hand until they are both evenly mixed through the dough.

Shape to fit a greased small (450-g/1-lb) loaf tin or

Opposite *Cheese Braid, Cheese and Onion Loaf
and Rolls (see page 39)*

Above *Cheese Rolls (see page 39)*

divide into 50-g/2-oz pieces and shape into rolls. Cover and prove. Bake the loaf in the centre of a hot oven (220°C., 425°F., Gas Mark 7) for 30–35 minutes and the rolls towards the top of the oven for 15–20 minutes. Sprinkle reserved cheese and onion on top 5 minutes before end of cooking time. Turn out and cool.

Herb Bread

Makes 1 small loaf or 8 rolls

METRIC/IMPERIAL
400 g/14 oz risen plain white dough
1 teaspoon dried mixed herbs or 2 tablespoons fresh
mixed herbs
TOPPING
15 g/½ oz butter
¼ teaspoon dried mixed herbs

Work the mixed herbs into the dough by squeezing and kneading the dough by hand until evenly mixed through the dough. Shape to fit a greased small (450-g/1-lb) loaf tin or divide into 50-g/2-oz pieces and shape into rolls.

Melt the butter and brush over the surface of the loaf or rolls. Sprinkle with the dried herbs. Cover and prove. Bake the loaf in the centre of a hot oven (220°C., 425°F., Gas Mark 7) for 30–35 minutes and the rolls towards the top of the oven for 15–20 minutes. Turn out and cool.

Currant Bread

METRIC/IMPERIAL
400 g/14 oz risen plain white dough
25 g/1 oz castor sugar
25 g/1 oz soft margarine or butter
50 g/2 oz currants

Work the sugar, fat and currants into the dough by squeezing and kneading the dough by hand until all the ingredients are evenly mixed through the dough. Shape to fit a well greased small (450-g/1-lb) loaf tin. Cover and prove.

Bake in the centre of a moderately hot oven (200°C., 400°F., Gas Mark 6) for about 35 minutes.

Remove from the tin and brush the top of the hot loaf with a wet brush dipped in honey or with a sugar glaze. Leave to cool.

Dough Cake

METRIC/IMPERIAL
350 g/12 oz risen plain white dough
50 g/2 oz soft butter or margarine
50 g/2 oz castor sugar
100 g/4 oz mixed dried fruit
¼ teaspoon grated nutmeg

Work the fat, sugar, dried fruit and grated nutmeg into the dough by squeezing and kneading by hand or with a mixer and beater until thoroughly mixed. This results

in a sticky dough. Turn the dough into a well greased small (450-g/1-lb) loaf tin and smooth the top. Cover and prove until the dough reaches the top of the tin.

(Rich mixtures such as this take longer to prove and it will probably take at least 1½ hours in a warm place, longer in a cool place.)

Bake in the centre of a moderately hot oven (200°C., 400°F., Gas Mark 6) for 35–40 minutes. Remove from the tin and brush the top of the hot loaf with a wet brush dipped in honey or with a sugar glaze. Leave to cool.

Orange Fruited Bun

METRIC/IMPERIAL
350 g/12 oz risen plain white dough
grated rind of ½ orange
50 g/2 oz currants
25 g/1 oz mixed peel
15 g/½ oz castor sugar

Work all the additional ingredients into the dough by squeezing and kneading together by hand or with a mixer and beater until thoroughly mixed. Shape into a round, 15 cm/6 inches across and 1 cm/½ inch thick, using floured hands, and place on a greased baking tray. Cover and prove. Bake towards the top of a moderately hot oven (200°C., 400°F., Gas Mark 6) for 25–30 minutes. Brush the top of the hot loaf with a wet brush dipped in honey or with a sugar glaze. Leave to cool.

VARIATIONS ON WHOLEWHEAT OR WHEATMEAL BREAD

Standard Method (see page 31) or Short-Time Method (see page 36)

Crunchy Peanut Bread

Makes 1 large or 2 small loaves or 18 rolls

METRIC/IMPERIAL
25 g/1 oz fresh yeast or 3 teaspoons dried yeast
1 tablespoon soft brown sugar
450 ml/¾ pint warm water
2 teaspoons yeast extract
100 g/4 oz crunchy peanut butter
675 g/1½ lb wholewheat flour
2 teaspoons salt
50 g/2 oz salted peanuts, chopped

Prepare as for Wholewheat Bread (see page 31) using 300 ml/½ pint warm water to dissolve the yeast and the remainder of the water to dissolve the yeast extract. Rub the peanut butter into the flour and salt, and add the chopped peanuts. Add both liquids to the dry ingredients.

Bake in the centre of a moderately hot oven (200°C., 400°F., Gas Mark 6) allowing 35–40 minutes for a large loaf and 30–35 minutes for small loaves. Bake rolls towards the top of the oven for 20 minutes. Turn out and cool.

Apricot and Walnut Loaf

METRIC/IMPERIAL
400 g/14 oz risen wholewheat or wheatmeal dough
50 g/2 oz dried apricots, chopped
50 g/2 oz walnuts, roughly chopped
2 tablespoons honey
25 g/1 oz soft margarine or butter

Put all the ingredients into a large basin. Squeeze and work the ingredients together by hand or with a mixer and beater until thoroughly mixed. Turn the mixture into a well greased small (450-g/1-lb) loaf tin. Smooth the top. Cover and prove until the dough reaches the top of the tin. This will take about 1½ hours in a warm place, longer in a cool place.

Bake in the centre of a moderately hot oven (200°C., 400°F., Gas Mark 6) for 30–35 minutes. Brush the hot loaf with a wet brush dipped in honey or with a sugar glaze after removing from the tin. Leave to cool.
Variation Replace the dried apricots with 50 g/2 oz chopped dates, sultanas or raisins.

Wholewheat or Wheatmeal Prune Bread

METRIC/IMPERIAL
400 g/14 oz risen wholewheat or wheatmeal dough
50 g/2 oz prunes
grated rind of ½ orange
25 g/1 oz soft brown sugar

Remove the stones and chop the prunes. Add to the dough in a bowl with the remaining ingredients. Proceed as for Apricot and Walnut Loaf.

Savoury Rolled Buns

Makes 9

These savoury buns are ideal to serve with salads or in packed or picnic lunches. They can be prepared from any of the following risen doughs: plain white, rich milk, tomato, onion or wholewheat.

METRIC/IMPERIAL
400 g/14 oz risen dough
15 g/½ oz butter or margarine
FILLING I
50 g/2 oz streaky bacon
25 g/1 oz onion, finely chopped
50 g/2 oz Cheddar cheese, grated
FILLING II
50 g/2 oz cooked ham, finely chopped
50 g/2 oz Cheddar cheese, grated
2 teaspoons dry mustard
2 teaspoons Worcestershire sauce

Roll out the dough to an oblong 15 cm/6 inches by 30 cm/12 inches. Melt the butter or margarine and use to brush the surface of the dough. Spread with the prepared filling.
Filling I Remove the rinds, chop the bacon and fry in a non-stick pan until cooked. Remove the bacon, allowing any fat to drain back into the pan. Fry the onion gently in the bacon fat until soft but not coloured. Mix the finely grated cheese with the bacon and onion.
Filling II Mix the ham, cheese, mustard and Worcestershire sauce together.

Roll the dough up tightly from the long edge as for a Swiss roll. Cut into 9 equal pieces and place cut side down in three rows of three in a greased 18-cm/7-inch square tin. Cover with oiled polythene and prove for 20–30 minutes in a warm place; the rolls should join up. Bake towards the top of a moderately hot oven (200°C., 400°F., Gas Mark 6) for about 25 minutes. Remove to a wire rack. Serve hot or cold, pulling apart to serve.

Treacle Loaf

A mixer and beater are very useful when making this bread since it is very sticky; however, it can be made by hand. The end result is certainly worth the stickiness, and treacle bread keeps well.

METRIC/IMPERIAL
400 g/14 oz risen wholewheat or wheatmeal dough
3 tablespoons black treacle
25 g/1 oz soft margarine

Put the risen dough, treacle and margarine into the bowl of a mixer or large basin. Mix with a beater or squeeze and mix thoroughly with one hand until the mixture is no longer streaky. Well grease and line the base of a small (450-g/1-lb) loaf tin. Add the mixture and smooth the top. Cover and prove until the dough reaches the top of the tin. This will take 1–2 hours in a warm place, longer in a cool place.

Bake in the centre of a moderately hot oven (200°C., 400°F., Gas Mark 6) for 30–35 minutes. Brush the hot loaf with a wet brush dipped in honey or with a sugar glaze after removing from the tin. Leave to cool.

Variations
Treacle and ginger loaf Add 2 teaspoons ground ginger with the black treacle and margarine.

Treacle and fruit loaf Add 50 g/2 oz of any of the following fruits to the dough: sultanas, raisins, chopped dried figs, chopped stoned dates or chopped stoned prunes.

Wholewheat or wheatmeal malt bread Reduce amount of black treacle to 1 tablespoon and add 1 tablespoon malt extract and 75 g/3 oz sultanas to the dough.

VARIATIONS ON RICH MILK BREAD

*Standard Method (see page 32) or Short-Time Method
(see page 34)
Recipes are given in this section for fancy shapes as
well as fillings for fruited and fancy breads and buns.*

Easter Bunnies

Makes 6

These are popular for Easter breakfast.

METRIC/IMPERIAL
350 g/12 oz risen rich milk dough
egg wash

Divide the dough into a 50-g/2-oz piece for each
bunny. Then cut each piece of dough in half. Roll one
half to a thin strand 25 cm/10 inches long, and coil up
loosely to form the body. Divide the other half in two
and roll one piece to a thin strand 13 cm/5 inches long.
Coil up loosely to form the head. Roll out the remaining
piece to form the two ears and a small ball for the tail.
Assemble these pieces in the shape of a rabbit on a
lightly greased baking tray. Repeat for other bunnies.

Cover and prove for about 30 minutes in a warm
place. Brush with egg wash. Bake towards the top of a
moderately hot oven (190°C., 375°F., Gas Mark 5) for
15–20 minutes. Cool on a wire rack.

Napkin Ring Rolls

Makes 6

METRIC/IMPERIAL
350 g/12 oz risen rich milk dough
egg wash

Divide the dough into a 50-g/2-oz piece for each roll.
Then cut each piece in half. Roll each half to a thin
strand 30 cm/12 inches long. Twist the 2 strands
together and join to form a circle. Place on a greased
baking tray. Repeat for the other rolls.

Cover and prove for about 30 minutes in a warm
place. Brush with egg wash. Bake towards the top of a
moderately hot oven (190°C., 375°F., Gas Mark 5) for
15–20 minutes. Cool on a wire rack and serve at dinner
with napkins threaded through the holes.

Ring Doughnuts

Makes 8

METRIC/IMPERIAL
425 g/15 oz risen rich milk dough
FINISH
50 g/2 oz castor sugar
½ teaspoon ground cinnamon

Divide the dough into 8 equal pieces. Roll each piece
into a ball, then make a large hole through the centre of
each using two fingers. Stretch out to make a circle. Put

the doughnuts on a greased baking tray. Cover and
prove until doubled in size.

Fill a deep-fat fryer to one-third full with cooking oil
and heat to 180°C. (360°F.). To test if it is ready without
a thermometer, drop in a cube of bread, which should
turn brown in 20 seconds. When the oil is ready, fry the
doughnuts a few at a time, for 2 minutes on each side.
Using a draining spoon, lift them out and drain on
absorbent kitchen paper.

Mix the sugar and cinnamon in a large paper bag
and toss the hot doughnuts in the mixture to coat them
evenly. Doughnuts should be eaten when fresh.

Jam Doughnuts

Makes 8

METRIC/IMPERIAL
425 g/15 oz risen rich milk dough
4 teaspoons jam
FINISH
50 g/2 oz castor sugar
½ teaspoon ground cinnamon

Divide the dough into 8 equal pieces. Roll each piece
into a ball and place on a greased baking tray. Cover
and prove for 20 minutes in a warm place. Make a hole
in the centre of each piece of dough and place ½
teaspoon jam in each hole. Pinch the dough round the
jam to re-form a ball. Cover and prove again for 15
minutes.

Fry and finish as for Ring Doughnuts.

Currant Whirl

METRIC/IMPERIAL
425 g/15 oz risen rich milk dough
15 g/½ oz butter or margarine
100 g/4 oz currants
25 g/1 oz castor sugar
1 teaspoon ground cinnamon

Roll out the dough on a lightly floured surface to a
rectangle 35 cm/14 inches by 13 cm/5 inches. Melt
the fat and brush over the surface. Mix the currants,
sugar and ground cinnamon together and sprinkle
evenly over the surface. Roll the dough up across the
width making a 35-cm/14-inch roll. Curl it into a well
greased 20-cm/8-inch round cake tin. Cover and
prove.

Brush the surface with milk and sprinkle lightly with
castor sugar. Bake in the centre of a moderately hot
oven (190°C., 375°F., Gas Mark 5) for 30–35 minutes.
Cool on a wire rack and serve cut into slices like a
cake.

Almond Christmas Wreath

METRIC/IMPERIAL
425 g/15 oz risen rich milk dough
100 g/4 oz marzipan
50 g/2 oz icing sugar
1 tablespoon orange juice
25 g/1 oz flaked almonds, toasted

Divide the dough into 2 pieces. Roll out each piece to a long rectangle about 30 cm/12 inches by 13 cm/5 inches. Divide the marzipan in half and roll each piece into a rectangle a little smaller than the dough. Place 1 piece on top of each rectangle of dough. Roll the dough up across the width making 30-cm/12-inch rolls and seal the edges of the dough. Twist the 2 pieces of dough together, form into a circle and seal the ends together. Place on a greased baking tray. Cover and prove.

Brush with egg wash and bake in the centre of a moderately hot oven (190°C., 375°F., Gas Mark 5) for 30–35 minutes. Remove to a wire rack and cool.

Mix the icing sugar with the orange juice to form a pouring icing. Spoon all over the bread and sprinkle with the toasted flaked almonds whilst the icing is still wet. Leave to set.

Christmas Tree Bread

METRIC/IMPERIAL
425 g/15 oz risen rich milk dough
225 g/8 oz mincemeat
FINISH
50 g/2 oz granulated sugar
2 tablespoons milk
25 g/1 oz butter
25 g/1 oz glacé cherries

Roll the dough to a rectangle 42 cm/17 inches by 20 cm/8 inches. Cut off a 2·5-cm/1-inch strip from one short end to make the trunk. Place the large rectangle on a greased baking tray. Mark the centre of one long edge and then mark two lines from this point to the corners on the opposite side of the dough. The middle (larger) triangle forms the main shape of the Christmas tree. Spread the mincemeat in this triangle and fold the uncovered parts of the dough down over the filling to meet in the middle and form a triangle. Make diagonal cuts down both long sides of the triangle with a sharp knife, 2·5 cm/1 inch apart and almost to the centre to form the boughs. Turn each bough over onto its side.

Roll up the strip of dough reserved for the trunk and place at the centre bottom. Cover and prove for about 30 minutes in a warm place.

Bake in the centre of a moderately hot oven (190°C., 375°F., Gas Mark 5) for 30–35 minutes. Remove to a wire rack and cool.

Prepare the finish by dissolving the sugar in the milk and butter over a low heat, then bringing up to the boil. Boil rapidly for 2 minutes. Spread the frosting over the boughs of the Christmas tree and decorate with glacé cherries.

Apricot Carousel Teabread

The filling of this teabread is improved if the dried apricots are soaked before using.

METRIC/IMPERIAL
425 g/15 oz risen rich milk dough
100 g/4 oz dried apricots
15 g/½ oz butter or margarine
25 g/1 oz almonds
25 g/1 oz castor sugar
½ teaspoon ground cinnamon

Cover the dried apricots with boiling water and leave to stand for 2 hours. Drain. Roll the dough to a rectangle 23 cm/9 inches by 30 cm/12 inches. Melt the butter or margarine in a small pan and brush all over the surface of the dough. Chop the soaked apricots and almonds and mix with the sugar and cinnamon. Sprinkle over the dough.

Roll the dough up tightly across the width making a 30-cm/12-inch roll. With a sharp knife cut the roll into 7 equal slices. Place 6 rolls cut side down round the outside of a greased 20-cm/8-inch round sandwich tin and 1 roll in the centre. Cover and prove for about 30 minutes in a warm place.

Bake in the centre of a moderately hot oven (190°C., 375°F., Gas Mark 5) for 25–30 minutes. Remove to a wire rack. Glaze the top of the hot loaf by brushing with a wet brush dipped in clear honey or with a sugar glaze. To serve, either pull rolls apart or slice like a cake.

Variation Replace the dried apricots with dried prunes.

Overleaf *Ring and Jam Doughnuts*

47

Butterscotch Buns

Makes 9

These are delicious sticky buns ideal for serving with coffee (but remember to have plenty of napkins for sticky fingers).

METRIC/IMPERIAL
425 g/15 oz risen rich milk dough
40 g/1½ oz butter
150 g/6 oz soft brown sugar
50 g/2 oz blanched almonds, chopped
2 teaspoons ground cinnamon

Roll the dough to a rectangle 23 cm/9 inches by 30 cm/12 inches. Melt the butter and use 15 g/½ oz to brush over the surface of the dough. Mix the remaining melted butter with 100 g/4 oz soft brown sugar and the almonds. Spread this mixture in the base of an 18-cm/7-inch well greased square cake tin. Mix the remaining 50 g/2 oz sugar with the ground cinnamon and sprinkle over the dough. Roll up tightly across the width making a 30-cm/12-inch roll and cut into 9 equal slices using a sharp knife. Place these, cut side down, on the butterscotch mixture in three rows of three.

Cover and prove for about 30 minutes in a warm place. Bake just above the centre of a moderately hot oven (190°C., 375°F., Gas Mark 5) for 25–30 minutes. Turn out onto a wire rack immediately after removing from oven. To serve, pull apart to separate rolls.

Honey, Date and Nut Buns

Makes 9

METRIC/IMPERIAL
425 g/15 oz risen rich milk dough
15 g/½ oz butter or margarine
100 g/4 oz stoned dates
25 g/1 oz walnuts
2 tablespoons honey
1 teaspoon grated lemon rind

Roll the dough to a rectangle 23 cm/9 inches by 30 cm/12 inches. Melt the butter or margarine in a small pan and brush over the surface of the dough. Chop the dates and walnuts and place in a small pan with the honey and lemon rind. Warm gently until the honey is well blended.

Spread this mixture over the dough. Roll up tightly across the width making a 30-cm/12-inch roll and cut into 9 equal slices using a sharp knife. Place, cut side down, well apart on a greased baking tray or into well greased tartlet tins. Cover and prove for about 30 minutes in a warm place.

Bake just above the centre of a moderately hot oven (190°C., 375°F., Gas Mark 5) for 20–25 minutes. Remove to a wire rack and glaze by brushing the tops of the buns with a wet brush dipped in clear honey or with a sugar glaze whilst still hot.
Variation Replace the dates with raisins or chopped glacé cherries.

Coffee and Chocolate Swirl

This is particularly popular with children and is ideal for replacing cake at tea time and is more economical (that is unless they like it so much that they eat more of it than they would cake!). It is also delicious with coffee.

METRIC/IMPERIAL
425 g/15 oz risen rich milk dough
1 tablespoon coffee essence
25 g/1 oz chocolate chips or drops
FINISH
75 g/3 oz icing sugar
1–2 tablespoons black coffee
25 g/1 oz walnuts, chopped

Place the dough in a basin and add the coffee essence and chocolate drops. Squeeze and knead together until evenly mixed and there are no white streaks remaining in the dough. Turn out onto a lightly floured surface and roll out to a 50-cm/20-inch strand.

Grease a 20-cm/8-inch sandwich tin and coil the dough round in the tin. Cover and prove for about 30 minutes in a warm place.

Bake in the centre of a moderately hot oven (190°C., 375°F., Gas Mark 5) for approximately 25 minutes. Remove from the tin and cool on a wire rack.

Decorate with coffee glacé icing made by mixing icing sugar and black coffee to give a soft icing, and sprinkle with chopped walnuts.

Tea Rings

Use 425 g/15 oz risen rich milk dough, 15 g/½ oz melted butter or margarine and any of the fillings and finishes given opposite.

Roll the dough to a rectangle 20 cm/8 inches by 35 cm/14 inches. Brush with melted butter or margarine and sprinkle or spread the filling over the dough. Roll up tightly across the width making a 35-cm/14-inch roll. Place on a greased baking tray. Bend round to form a ring and pinch the ends together to seal.

Using scissors, cut through the dough at an angle to within 1 cm/½ inch of the centre. Repeat all round the circle at 2·5-cm/1-inch intervals. Turn the cut sections on their sides. Cover and prove for about 30 minutes in a warm place.

Bake in the centre of a moderately hot oven (190°C., 375°F., Gas Mark 5) for 30–35 minutes. Remove to a wire rack, cool and finish.

Swedish Tea Ring

METRIC / IMPERIAL
FILLING
50 g / 2 oz soft brown sugar
2 teaspoons ground cinnamon
FINISH
75 g / 3 oz icing sugar
1–2 tablespoons cold water
4 glacé cherries
4 walnut halves

For the filling mix the brown sugar and cinnamon together, and then sprinkle evenly over the dough.

For the finish sieve the icing sugar and mix with sufficient cold water to give a soft consistency. Spoon over the top of the baked, cooled tea ring and allow to run down the sides. Roughly chop the cherries and walnuts and sprinkle them over the icing before it sets.

Almond Tea Ring

METRIC / IMPERIAL
FILLING
50 g / 2 oz castor sugar
50 g / 2 oz ground almonds
2 tablespoons egg white
FINISH
75 g / 3 oz icing sugar
1–2 tablespoons orange juice
4 glacé cherries
small strip of angelica

For the filling mix the sugar and almonds with sufficient egg white to form a soft paste, then spread over the dough.

For the finish sieve the icing sugar and mix with sufficient orange juice to give a soft consistency. Spoon over the top of the baked, cooled tea ring and allow to run down the sides. Halve the glacé cherries and cut the angelica into 16 small diamonds. Decorate the iced ring with cherries and angelica before the icing sets.

Gala Tea Ring

METRIC / IMPERIAL
FILLING
25 g / 1 oz walnuts
25 g / 1 oz glacé cherries
25 g / 1 oz seedless raisins
25 g / 1 oz soft brown sugar
1 teaspoon ground cinnamon
FINISH
75 g / 3 oz icing sugar
1–2 tablespoons lemon juice
25 g / 1 oz walnuts, chopped
small strip of angelica

For the filling chop the walnuts and cherries. Mix all the ingredients together and sprinkle over the dough.

For the finish sieve the icing sugar and mix with sufficient lemon juice to give a soft consistency. Spoon over the top of the baked, cooled tea ring and allow to run down the sides. Decorate before icing sets.

Sweet and Savoury Braids

Use 425 g / 15 oz risen rich milk dough, 15 g / ½ oz melted butter or margarine and any of the fillings and finishes given overleaf.

Roll the dough to a rectangle 23 cm / 9 inches by 30 cm / 12 inches. Place on a greased baking tray and brush with melted fat. Spread filling down the centre.

Using a sharp knife make diagonal cuts about 5 cm / 2 inches apart down the remaining dough on both sides. Take a strip at a time from alternate sides and cross them over the filling to give the top a plaited effect. Cover and prove for about 30 minutes in a warm place. Bake in the centre of a moderately hot oven (190°C., 375°F., Gas Mark 5) for 25–30 minutes.

Overleaf Gala Tea Ring, Swedish Tea Ring and Almond Tea Ring

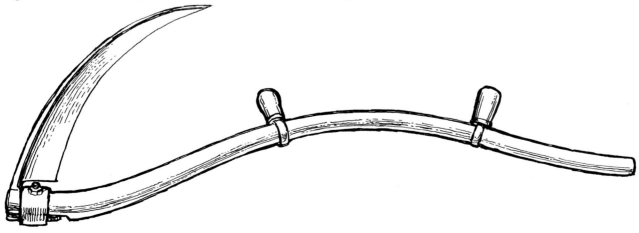

Variations

Apple and Raisin Braid

METRIC/IMPERIAL
FILLING
2 medium cooking apples
50 g/2 oz seedless raisins
50 g/2 oz soft brown sugar
½ teaspoon ground cinnamon
FINISH
50 g/2 oz castor sugar
2 tablespoons milk

For the filling peel, core and chop the apples and put them into a pan with raisins, sugar and cinnamon. Cook over a low heat for about 10–15 minutes or until the apple is soft. Leave to cool.

For the finish put the sugar and milk into a small pan and dissolve the sugar over a low heat, then bring the liquid to the boil and boil it rapidly for 2 minutes. Brush the glaze over the baked, cooled braid.

Cherry and Walnut Braid

METRIC/IMPERIAL
FILLING
50 g/2 oz butter
50 g/2 oz walnuts
50 g/2 oz glacé cherries
50 g/2 oz dried browned breadcrumbs
4 tablespoons clear honey
FINISH
75 g/3 oz icing sugar
2 tablespoons water

For the filling melt the butter, and chop the walnuts and the cherries. Mix with the breadcrumbs and honey.

For the finish sieve the icing sugar and mix with sufficient cold water to give a soft consistency. Spread over the top of the baked, cooled braid.

Date Braid

METRIC/IMPERIAL
FILLING
225 g/8 oz stoned dates
2 tablespoons lemon juice
FINISH
25 g/1 oz sugar lumps
milk

For the filling chop the dates and place in a small saucepan. Make the lemon juice up to 150 ml/¼ pint with water. Add to the dates and bring to the boil, stirring continuously. Cook gently for about 5 minutes, stirring occasionally until the dates are pulped. Leave to cool before using.

For the finish place the sugar lumps in a paper bag and lightly crush with a rolling pin. Before baking brush the risen braid with milk and sprinkle with the crushed sugar lumps.

Sausage Braid

METRIC/IMPERIAL
FILLING
1 small onion, peeled and chopped
225 g/8 oz pork sausagemeat
15 g/½ oz lard
1 teaspoon chopped fresh parsley
½ teaspoon dried mixed herbs
25 g/1 oz fresh breadcrumbs
salt and pepper to taste
FINISH
milk or egg wash

For the filling mix the onion with the sausagemeat. Melt the lard and fry the sausagemeat and onion in it gently for 5 minutes. Remove from the heat and add the remainder of the ingredients and mix well. Leave to cool before using.

For the finish brush the surface of the braid before baking with milk or egg wash.
Note Wholewheat and wheatmeal doughs are also excellent in this recipe. Use the same amount of the chosen risen dough in place of rich milk dough.

Ham and Mushroom Braid

METRIC/IMPERIAL
FILLING
1 small onion, peeled and chopped
25 g/1 oz lard or dripping
100 g/4 oz mushrooms, chopped
100 g/4 oz cooked ham, diced
25 g/1 oz fresh breadcrumbs
salt and pepper to taste
¼ teaspoon dry mustard
½ teaspoon Worcestershire sauce
1 egg, beaten
FINISH
milk or egg wash

For the filling lightly fry the onion in the lard or dripping for 1–2 minutes. Add the mushrooms and ham and fry until the onion is soft but not coloured. Remove from the heat and add the breadcrumbs, seasonings and sauce and bind with the beaten egg. Leave to cool before using.

For the finish brush the surface of the braid before baking with milk or egg wash.
Note Wholewheat and wheatmeal doughs are also excellent in this recipe. Use the same amount of the chosen risen dough in place of rich milk dough.

Rich Fruit Bread Dough

Dried fruits and nuts and a little grated orange or lemon rind may be added to the basic Rich Milk Bread recipe to give a delicious rich fruit bread. The 'Standard' or 'Short-Time' Method may be used but the final proving time will be increased for either method since the additional ingredients slow down the rising or proving. Additional ingredients to the basic recipe are given below.

METRIC/IMPERIAL
100 g/4 oz currants
100 g/4 oz sultanas
25 g/1 oz chopped mixed peel
25 g/1 oz walnuts or almonds, chopped (optional)
2 teaspoons grated orange or lemon rind

Standard Method Follow the method as for Rich Milk Bread (see page 32) adding the additional ingredients with the dry ingredients to the yeast batter.
Short-Time Method Follow the method as for Rich Milk Bread (see page 34) adding the additional ingredients to the dry ingredients before adding the yeast liquid.

Variations

Rich Fruit Loaves

Makes 2 small loaves

METRIC/IMPERIAL
850 g/1 lb 14 oz risen rich fruit bread dough

Divide the dough into 2 equal pieces. Shape to fit two well greased small (450-g/1-lb) loaf tins. Cover and prove about 45 minutes to 1 hour in a warm place.

Bake in the centre of a moderately hot oven (190°C., 375°F., Gas Mark 5) for 30–35 minutes. Remove the loaves from the tins and whilst still hot brush with a wet brush dipped in clear honey or with a sugar glaze.

Overleaf *Ham and Mushroom Braid and Sausage Braid*

Stollen

METRIC/IMPERIAL
425 g/15 oz risen rich fruit bread dough
15 g/½ oz butter
50 g/2 oz glacé cherries, chopped

Mould dough to an oval shape 30 cm/12 inches by 20 cm/8 inches. Brush with melted butter and spread chopped glacé cherries over one half. Fold the other half over the cherries and press down lightly. Cover and prove for about 45 minutes to 1 hour in a warm place. Remove cover and brush the top with melted butter. Bake in the centre of a moderately hot oven (190°C., 375°F., Gas Mark 5) for 20–25 minutes. Remove to a wire tray, cool and dust with sieved icing sugar.

Fruit Twist

METRIC/IMPERIAL
425 g/15 oz risen rich fruit bread dough
100 g/4 oz icing sugar
2 tablespoons lemon juice
25 g/1 oz flaked almonds, toasted

Divide dough into 2 pieces. Roll each piece to a strand 35 cm/14 inches long. Follow the instructions for shaping a twist (see page 32). Cover and prove for about 45 minutes to 1 hour in a warm place. Remove cover and brush with egg wash.

Bake in the centre of a moderately hot oven (190°C., 375°F., Gas Mark 5) for 25–30 minutes. Remove to a wire rack.
Finish I Brush the hot loaf with a wet brush dipped in honey or with a sugar glaze.
Finish II Blend icing sugar with lemon juice to give a pouring consistency. Spoon over the top of the cooled loaf, allowing the icing to run down the sides. Sprinkle toasted flaked almonds over the top.

VARIATIONS ON SWEET BREAD

Standard Method or Short-Time Method (see page 35)

Orange Rosette Buns

Makes 12

METRIC/IMPERIAL
425 g/15 oz risen sweet bread dough
15 g/½ oz butter or margarine, melted
50 g/2 oz castor sugar
1 tablespoon grated orange rind

Roll the dough to a rectangle 20 cm/8 inches by 45 cm/18 inches. Brush all over with the melted fat. Mix the sugar and grated orange rind together and sprinkle over the dough.

Fold over in thirds to form a rectangle 20 cm/8 inches by 15 cm/6 inches. With a sharp knife cut into 12 equal strips 15 cm/6 inches long. Roll the ends of each strip in opposite directions and bring together to form a circle. Seal the ends and place buns well apart on a greased baking tray.

Cover and prove for about 30 minutes in a warm place. Bake towards the top of a moderately hot oven (190°C., 375°F., Gas Mark 5) for 15–20 minutes. Remove to a wire rack and cool.

Currant Buns

Makes 8

METRIC/IMPERIAL
425 g/15 oz risen sweet bread dough
50 g/2 oz currants

Work the currants into the dough by squeezing and kneading until evenly mixed. Divide the dough into 8 equal pieces. Roll into buns using the palm of one hand. Do not overwork the dough; a little oil on the palm of the hand and on the working surface will help to give a smooth finish.

Place well apart on a greased baking tray. Cover and prove for about 45 minutes in a warm place. Bake towards the top of a moderately hot oven (190°C., 375°F., Gas Mark 5) for approximately 20 minutes. Remove buns to a wire rack, brush the warm buns with a sugar glaze and leave to cool.
Note Wholewheat or wheatmeal doughs make good alternatives.

Jam Buns

Makes 8

METRIC/IMPERIAL
425 g/15 oz risen sweet bread dough
1 teaspoon grated lemon rind
4 teaspoons jam

Work lemon rind evenly into the dough. Divide into 8 equal pieces. Roll into buns. Place well apart on a greased baking tray. Cover and prove for 20 minutes.

Press the handle of a wooden spoon down into the centre of each bun to form a hole. Place a small quantity of jam (about ½ teaspoon) in the hole and pinch the dough round it to re-form the bun. Cover and prove for a further 15–20 minutes. Bake towards the top of a moderately hot oven (190°C., 375°F., Gas Mark 5) for 15–20 minutes. Remove to a wire rack and cool.

Jam Crescents

Makes 8

METRIC/IMPERIAL
425 g/15 oz risen sweet bread dough
1 teaspoon grated lemon rind
15 g/½ oz butter or margarine
4 teaspoons jam

Work the grated lemon rind evenly into the dough. Roll into a circle 5 mm/¼ inch thick and approximately 30 cm/12 inches in diameter. Cut into 8 triangles. Brush each triangle with melted butter or margarine.

Put a little jam on the outer (short) edge of each triangle and roll up starting at the same edge. Bend into a crescent shape and tuck the end underneath.

Place well apart on greased baking trays. Cover and prove for about 30 minutes in a warm place. Remove cover and brush with egg wash. Bake towards the top of a moderately hot oven (190°C., 375°F., Gas Mark 5) for 15–20 minutes. Remove to a wire rack and cool.

Swiss Buns

Makes 6

METRIC/IMPERIAL
425 g/15 oz risen sweet bread dough
FINISH
175 g/6 oz icing sugar
2–3 tablespoons cold water

Divide the risen dough into 6 equal pieces and roll each piece into a sausage shape about 13 cm/5 inches long. Place well apart on a well greased baking tray. Cover and prove until doubled in size. Bake in the centre of a moderately hot oven (190°C., 375°F., Gas Mark 5) for 15–20 minutes. Remove to a wire rack and cool. Sieve the icing sugar and mix with sufficient cold water to give a fairly stiff icing. Dip the buns into the icing so that the tops are evenly covered. Leave to set.

Bun Round

Delicious sweet fruit bread baked in a round shape.

METRIC/IMPERIAL
425 g/15 oz risen sweet bread dough
50 g/2 oz sultanas
25 g/1 oz chopped mixed peel

Work the sultanas and mixed peel into the risen dough by squeezing and kneading until evenly mixed. Form the fruited dough into a 15-cm/6-inch round and lift onto a greased baking tray. Brush the surface with egg wash and mark it into 8 pieces using a sharp knife. Cover and prove.

Bake in the centre of a moderately hot oven (190°C., 375°F., Gas Mark 5) for 25–30 minutes. Cool on a wire rack and serve sliced and buttered.

Apricot Plait

METRIC/IMPERIAL
425 g/15 oz risen sweet bread dough
100 g/4 oz dried apricots
2 teaspoons grated lemon rind

Chop the dried apricots and work into the risen dough with the lemon rind by squeezing and kneading until evenly mixed. Divide into 3 equal pieces. Roll each piece into a strand approximately 35 cm/14 inches long. Pinch the 3 strands together at one end. Plait the strands evenly and pinch the remaining ends together. Place on a greased baking tray.

Cover and prove. Brush with egg wash. Bake in the centre of a moderately hot oven (190°C., 375°F., Gas Mark 5) for 25–30 minutes. Remove to a wire rack and leave to cool.

Overleaf Orange Bread (see page 62) with currants, Orange and Sultana Twist (page 63) and Cinnamon Orange Swirl (page 63)

59

Orange Bread

The best orange flavour is produced when the minced or liquidised shell of the orange, i.e. that which remains after the juice has been squeezed out, is used. However, for those who have neither mincer nor liquidiser the grated rind and juice may be used, which gives a pleasant flavour but a slightly sticky dough. Following this recipe for orange bread are variations using the orange bread dough since it so readily lends itself to alternative treatments.

METRIC/IMPERIAL
425 g/15 oz risen sweet bread dough
1 small or ½ large orange shell
or
2 tablespoons grated orange rind and
2 tablespoons orange juice

Mince or liquidise and add the orange shell or alternatively the grated orange rind and juice to the dough in a bowl. Work into the dough by squeezing and kneading until it is thoroughly and evenly mixed. Shape the dough to fit a well greased small (450-g/1-lb) loaf tin. Cover and prove. Bake in the centre of a moderately hot oven (190°C., 375°F., Gas Mark 5) for 30–35 minutes. Remove from the tin and brush the top of the hot baked loaf with a wet brush dipped in honey or with a sugar glaze.

Variations

Coiled Orange Loaf

METRIC/IMPERIAL
425 g/15 oz risen orange bread dough
FINISH
15 g/½ oz butter
25 g/1 oz icing sugar
2 teaspoons honey

Roll the orange bread dough out to a strand 35 cm/14 inches long. Coil round the inside of a well greased 20-cm/8-inch sandwich tin. Cover and prove.

Brush the surface of the loaf with a glaze prepared by melting together the butter, icing sugar and honey. Bake in the centre of a moderately hot oven (190°C., 375°F., Gas Mark 5) for 30 minutes. The glaze will turn golden brown during baking and no further glaze is required afterwards. Remove to a wire rack and cool.

To serve, cut into slices like a cake and serve with butter.

Cinnamon Orange Swirl

METRIC/IMPERIAL
425 g/15 oz risen orange bread dough
15 g/½ oz butter or margarine
FILLING
25 g/1 oz soft brown sugar
2 teaspoons ground cinnamon
FINISH
100 g/4 oz icing sugar
2 tablespoons orange juice

Roll the orange bread dough to a rectangle 15 cm/6 inches by 32 cm/13 inches. Melt the butter or margarine and brush all over the surface of the dough. Mix the brown sugar and cinnamon together and sprinkle over the dough. Roll up from the short edge to give a 15-cm/6-inch roll.

Place in a greased small (450-g/1-lb) loaf tin. Cover and prove for about 45 minutes in a warm place. Bake in the centre of a moderately hot oven (190°C., 375°F., Gas Mark 5) for 30–35 minutes. Cool on a wire rack.

Sieve the icing sugar and mix with the orange juice to give a thick icing. Spread evenly over the top of the loaf and leave to set.

Orange and Apricot Bread

METRIC/IMPERIAL
425 g/15 oz risen orange bread dough
50 g/2 oz dried apricots

Chop the apricots and work into the risen dough by squeezing and kneading until evenly mixed. Shape to fit a well greased small (450-g/1-lb) loaf tin. Cover and prove for about 1 hour in a warm place.

Bake in the centre of a moderately hot oven (190°C., 375°F., Gas Mark 5) for 30–35 minutes. Turn out onto a wire rack and brush the hot baked loaf with a wet brush dipped in honey or with a sugar glaze if liked.

Orange Flower Bread

METRIC/IMPERIAL
425 g/15 oz risen orange bread dough
FINISH
100 g/4 oz icing sugar
1 tablespoon grated orange rind
2 tablespoons orange juice

Grease a large baking tray and a 20-cm/8-inch flan ring, and stand the flan ring in the centre of the tray. Turn the dough into the flan ring and press it out evenly to the sides. Take off the flan ring and place a plain 7·5-cm/3-inch round biscuit cutter in the centre of the dough. Using a sharp knife, cut through the dough from the outside edge of the dough to the edge of the cutter at about 2·5-cm/1-inch intervals. Replace the flan ring, then taking each strip of dough separately, twist it twice and lay it down in the same place again. Cover and prove.
(It will rise above the top of the flan ring when fully proved.)

Brush with egg wash. Bake in the centre of a moderately hot oven (190°C., 375°F., Gas Mark 5) for about 30 minutes. Remove the flan ring to a wire rack and cool.

Sieve the icing sugar and mix with the grated orange rind and orange juice. Pour the icing into the centre of the bread and leave it to run down the sides.

Orange and Sultana Twist

METRIC/IMPERIAL
425 g/15 oz risen orange bread dough
100 g/4 oz sultanas
2 tablespoons orange juice
FINISH
100 g/4 oz icing sugar
2 tablespoons orange juice

Place the sultanas and 2 tablespoons orange juice in a small basin; leave to soak for 10 minutes. Drain the sultanas. Work the sultanas into the orange dough by squeezing and kneading until evenly mixed. Divide the dough into 2 pieces. Roll each piece to a strand 35 cm/14 inches long. Cross the 2 strands at the centre to form a cross. Take the two ends of the bottom strand and cross them over in the centre. Repeat this with the two ends of the other strand. Cross each strand alternately, building the twist vertically until all the dough is used up. Finally pinch the ends together and lay the twist on its side on a greased baking tray. Cover and prove. Remove cover and brush with egg wash. Bake in a moderately hot oven (190°C., 375°F., Gas Mark 5) for 25–30 minutes. Remove to a wire rack and cool.

Sieve the icing sugar and blend with 2 tablespoons orange juice to give a pouring consistency. Spoon over the top of the twist.

Chapter 5
Traditional Breads

A collection of traditional bread recipes from England, Ireland, Scotland and Wales has been made for this chapter. Breadmaking is a very old craft, and hence there are many traditional recipes, the better known of which have been included.

As some of these recipes are from times when kitchens and equipment were larger than today and so recipe quantities were often large, it has been necessary to adapt them to quantities conveniently made today. It has also been necessary, in some cases, to adapt the method for modern techniques. However, much care has been taken to ensure that the baked goods resemble closely the traditional baked goods and that they taste every bit as delicious.

Harvest Sheaf

Bread baked in the shape of a harvest sheaf is traditionally prepared for the church on Thanksgiving Sunday.

METRIC/IMPERIAL
2·25 kg/5 lb (double the basic recipe) risen plain
white dough (see page 30)
egg wash

Divide the dough into 4 equal pieces. Use one quarter and keep the remainder covered. Roll this piece of dough into a 'keyhole' shape, approximately 38 cm/15 inches high and 35 cm/14 inches across the 'hole'. Place on a greased baking tray and brush with egg wash. Take another piece, and half of the third piece of the dough, and divide into 20 pieces. Roll each piece into a thin strand to form the stalks. Place on the base from the centre of the 'hole' to the bottom.

Brush with egg wash to secure. Divide the remaining half of the third piece of dough into 2 and roll out to 2 strands about 35 cm/14 inches long. Twist together and wrap round the stalks about two-thirds of the way up to form the 'tie'.

Take the fourth piece of dough and roll out to 5 mm/¼ inch thick. Cut into 2·5-cm/1-inch diamond shapes. Snip each piece with the points of a pair of scissors to form the wheat ears. Arrange these in overlapping rows over the top of the base shape to give the appearance of wheat ears in a wheat sheaf. Secure by brushing with egg wash.

Brush the whole loaf with egg wash again. Cover and rest for 20 minutes. Bake in the centre of a hot oven (220°C., 425°F., Gas Mark 7) for 40–45 minutes. Cool on wire racks.

Note If the bread is not to be eaten but is to be used only as a decoration, it is best to let it dry out very slowly (to prevent cracking) in a cool oven so that mould does not develop.

Potato Bread

Makes 2 small loaves

Potatoes were used mostly as a food for the yeast during rising; however, they also give a good flavour and a moist loaf which keeps well. Prepare the mashed potatoes in the usual way with milk, butter and pepper. Nowadays, instant mashed potatoes may also be used.

METRIC/IMPERIAL
450 g/1 lb strong white flour
2 teaspoons castor sugar
15 g/½ oz fresh yeast or 1½ teaspoons dried yeast
200 ml/8 fl oz warm milk and water mixed
100 g/4 oz mashed potatoes
2 tablespoons oil
2 teaspoons salt

Prepare yeast batter: mix 100 g/4 oz flour, the sugar, the fresh or dried yeast and warm liquid together in a large bowl. Cover and set aside until frothy for about 20 minutes in a warm place, longer in a cool one. Mix the mashed potatoes, oil and salt into the batter and add sufficient of the remaining flour to mix to a firm dough.

Turn the dough onto a lightly floured surface and knead until smooth and elastic. It will take about 10 minutes by hand or 2–3 minutes with a mixer and dough hook. Shape the dough into a ball and place in an oiled polythene bag and leave to rise until doubled in size. Turn the risen dough onto a lightly floured surface, knock-back and knead until the dough is firm, for about 2 minutes.

Divide into 2 pieces and shape to fit two well greased small (450-g/1-lb) loaf tins. Cover and prove. Bake in the centre of a hot oven (230°C., 450°F., Gas Mark 8) for about 25 minutes. The crust should be deep brown in colour. Turn onto a wire rack to cool.

Oatmeal Bread

Clapbread

Makes 2 small loaves

This is an old English bread, particularly popular in Lancashire, prepared from a mixture of fine or medium oatmeal and wheat flour. It goes particularly well with cheese.

METRIC/IMPERIAL
225 g/8 oz fine or medium oatmeal
300 ml/½ pint milk
25 g/1 oz fresh yeast or 3 teaspoons dried yeast
1 teaspoon castor sugar
50 ml/2 fl oz warm water
350 g/12 oz strong white flour
2 teaspoons salt
2 tablespoons oil, melted butter or margarine

Soak the oatmeal in the milk for 30 minutes. Prepare yeast liquid: blend the fresh yeast in warm water until dissolved or dissolve the sugar in the warm water and sprinkle in the dried yeast. Leave in a warm place for 10 minutes or until dissolved and frothy.

Mix the soaked oatmeal, flour, salt and oil or melted fat together. Add the yeast liquid and mix to form a scone-like dough, adding extra flour if necessary. Turn the dough onto a lightly floured surface and knead until smooth and elastic and no longer sticky, about 10 minutes by hand.

Shape the dough into a ball and place in an oiled polythene bag and leave to rise until doubled in size. Remove from the polythene bag, knock-back and knead until the dough is firm, about 2 minutes. Divide into 2 pieces and shape each piece into a cob. Place on a floured baking tray. Cover and prove.

Brush the tops of the loaves with milk or salt water and sprinkle with oatmeal. Bake in the centre of a hot oven (230°C., 450°F., Gas Mark 8) for about 25 minutes. Remove to a wire rack and cool.
Variation Shape and place in two small (450-g/1-lb) loaf tins. Bake as above for 30 minutes.

White Soda Bread

Soda bread, the traditional bread of Ireland, is quick and easy to make. It does not keep well unless frozen.

METRIC/IMPERIAL
450 g/1 lb plain white flour
1 teaspoon salt
1 teaspoon sugar (optional)
25 g/1 oz lard or margarine
USING SOUR MILK
2 teaspoons bread soda
300 ml/½ pint soured or buttermilk
USING FRESH MILK
2 teaspoons baking powder
300 ml/½ pint fresh milk

Sieve the flour and salt into a bowl, add the sugar, then rub in the fat until the mixture resembles fine breadcrumbs. Make a 'well' in the centre and add the milk mixture, all at once. Stir and mix together to form a soft dough, adding a little extra milk if necessary.

Turn onto a floured surface and knead lightly until smooth. Form into a round about 5 cm/2 inches thick and place in a greased 18-cm/7-inch cake tin. Cut a deep cross on top, or 3 parallel lines, using a sharp knife.

Bake in the centre of a hot oven (220°C., 425°F., Gas Mark 7) for the first 10 minutes. Reduce the temperature to moderately hot (200°C., 400°F., Gas Mark 6) and continue for a further 30 minutes. The bread is ready if the base sounds hollow when tapped.

To prevent the crust from becoming hard during baking, cover over the top of the bread with kitchen foil when the top is sufficiently brown. Rub over the baked bread with a little margarine or butter, or wrap, while hot, in a clean dry tea towel.

Oxfordshire Lardy Cake

METRIC/IMPERIAL
550 g/1¼ lb (½ basic recipe) risen plain white dough
(see page 30)
175 g/6 oz lard
175 g/6 oz granulated sugar
¼ teaspoon grated nutmeg, ground cinnamon or
allspice

Roll the dough to a long rectangle 5 mm/¼ inch thick. Dot one-third of the cold, firm lard in little pats all over the dough. Sprinkle with one-third of the sugar then fold into three, pinching the sides together to keep in the air. Roll out to a strip again and repeat the lard, sugar and rolling process twice more but also sprinkling with the spice before folding. (Sprinkle the spice very delicately because the lard takes up the aroma strongly.) Roll out to fit a well greased 20-cm/8-inch square baking tin. Mark across the top to give a criss-

cross effect using a very sharp knife.

(It is traditional to break the lardy cake down its cracks and not to cut when serving.)

Cover and prove in a warm place for 30 minutes. Bake in the centre of a hot oven (230°C., 450°F., Gas Mark 8) for about 30 minutes. Remove from the tin and spoon any syrup remaining in the tin over the surface of the cake. Cool.

Wiltshire Lardy Cake

METRIC/IMPERIAL
400 g / 14 oz (⅓ basic recipe) risen plain white dough (see page 30)
100 g / 4 oz Wiltshire lard
100 g / 4 oz granulated sugar
100 g / 4 oz mixed sultanas and currants
½ teaspoon mixed spice (optional)
GLAZE
25 g / 1 oz granulated sugar
2 tablespoons milk

Roll the dough into a rectangle about 25 cm / 10 inches by 15 cm / 6 inches. Spread two-thirds of the dough with one-third of the lard and sprinkle with one-third of the sugar. Fold the uncovered third of dough up and the top third down. Seal the edges by pressing with a rolling pin. Give a half turn to the dough and roll out as above again. Repeat this process twice more but add the fruit and spice (if used) each time with the lard and sugar.

Roll out and fold once more without any additions then roll to fit an 18-cm / 7-inch square cake tin which has been well greased with lard. Cover and prove in a warm place for 30 minutes.

Before baking score the top in a criss-cross pattern. Bake in the centre of a hot oven (230°C., 450°F., Gas Mark 8) for 25–30 minutes.

Prepare the glaze by dissolving the sugar in the milk and boiling for a few minutes until syrupy. Brush the glaze over the hot lardy cake. Remove cake from the tin and turn upside down. Spoon any lard or syrup left in tin over the cake. Serve upside down.

Opposite *White Soda Bread*
Below *Wiltshire Lardy Cake*

Saffron 'Cake' Bread

Makes 2 loaves or cakes

Traditional in the West Country, this is a saffron bread or dough cake. The saffron stamens are steeped in warm water in a covered jar. The water is drained off and used to mix the dough, which acquires a golden yellow colour. The original saffron cake was not sweet though strongly aromatic; however, today it is usually preferred sweet and containing dried fruit. Saffron may usually be obtained from a chemist.

METRIC/IMPERIAL
5 grains saffron
150 ml/¼ pint hot water
15 g/½ oz fresh yeast or 1½ teaspoons dried yeast
1 teaspoon castor sugar
300 ml/½ pint warm milk and water mixed
675 g/1½ lb strong white flour
1 teaspoon salt
75 g/3 oz lard
50 g/2 oz castor sugar
75 g/3 oz currants
75 g/3 oz sultanas
50 g/2 oz chopped mixed peel
½ teaspoon grated nutmeg

Put the saffron in the hot water, cover and leave to stand in a warm place overnight.

Prepare the yeast liquid: blend the fresh yeast in the warm milk and water or dissolve 1 teaspoon sugar in the warm liquid and sprinkle in the dried yeast. Leave to stand until frothy, about 10 minutes in a warm place.

Put the flour and salt in a large bowl and rub in the fat until the mixture resembles breadcrumbs. Stir in the sugar, dried fruit, peel and nutmeg. Drain the liquid from the saffron and add to the dry ingredients with the yeast liquid and mix well to form a soft dough. Cover the dough in the bowl and leave to rise in a warm place until doubled in size. (This may take 2 hours.)

Turn out of the bowl, knock-back and knead the dough until smooth and firm. Divide into 2 pieces and shape to fit two well greased 15-cm/6-inch round cake tins. Cover the tins and stand in a warm place until the dough has risen to the top of the tins. Bake in the centre of a moderately hot oven (200°C., 400°F., Gas Mark 6) for 35–40 minutes. Turn out and cool on a wire rack.

Good Friday Caraway Bread

It was the general custom in certain areas of the South West, particularly Somerset, to make a batch of caraway bread on Good Friday. This special bread made on this day was supposed to keep good for seven years; in fact, it was never allowed to since it was too good to keep.

METRIC/IMPERIAL
15 g/½ oz fresh yeast or 1½ teaspoons dried yeast
1 teaspoon castor sugar
300 ml/½ pint warm water or milk and water mixed
450 g/1 lb strong white flour
1 teaspoon salt
25 g/1 oz butter or margarine
25 g/1 oz castor sugar
1½ teaspoons caraway seeds

Follow the method for Plain White Bread (Standard Method) (see page 30), adding the sugar and caraway seeds to the flour before forming into a dough. Shape into one large cob and brush with milk. Cover and prove until doubled in size. Bake in the centre of a moderately hot oven (200°C., 400°F., Gas Mark 6) for 40–45 minutes. Cool on a wire rack.

Lakeland Christmas Bread and Cakes

Makes 1 large or 2 small loaves and 10 cakes

A rich, dark fruit bread, traditional in Lakeland. Usually served cold with butter and cheese on Christmas Eve, but will keep over the Christmas holiday and tastes delicious when warmed in the oven (wrapped in foil), sliced and buttered.

METRIC/IMPERIAL
800 g/1¾ lb strong white flour
1 teaspoon castor sugar
25 g/1 oz fresh yeast or 3 teaspoons dried yeast
150 ml/¼ pint boiling water
200 ml/8 fl oz cold milk
1 teaspoon salt
75 g/3 oz lard
175 g/6 oz soft brown or castor sugar
100 g/4 oz currants
225 g/8 oz raisins
100 g/4 oz sultanas
50 g/2 oz chopped mixed peel
1 teaspoon mixed spice
2 standard eggs
1 tablespoon black treacle

Prepare the yeast batter: mix 225 g/8 oz flour, 1 teaspoon of sugar, and the fresh or dried yeast together in a large bowl. Add the boiling water to the milk and mix well into the yeast mixture. Cover and set aside until frothy, about 20 minutes in a warm place but longer in a cool one. Mix the remaining flour with the salt and rub in the fat until the mixture resembles breadcrumbs. Stir in the sugar, dried fruit, peel and mixed spice. Beat the eggs and treacle together, add with the dry ingredients to the yeast batter and mix well to give a soft dough, adding extra flour if the dough is too sticky to handle.

Turn the dough onto a lightly floured surface and knead until smooth, about 10 minutes by hand or 2–3 minutes with a mixer and dough hook. Shape the dough into a ball and place inside a large greased bowl, cover and put to rise until doubled in size, about 2 hours in a warm place. Turn the risen dough onto a lightly floured surface, knock-back and knead until the dough is firm, about 2 minutes.

Divide into 2 pieces. Use one half to make one large loaf, or divide into 2 again and make two small loaves. Shape the dough to fit one large (1-kg/2-lb) well greased loaf tin or two small (450-g/1-lb) well greased loaf tins. Use the remaining half of the dough to make cakes. Divide into 10 equal pieces and roll each piece into a ball. Then roll each one out slightly with a rolling pin and place well apart on a greased baking tray. Cover loaves and cakes and put to rise until doubled in size.

Bake loaves in the centre and cakes towards the top of a moderately hot oven (190°C., 375°F., Gas Mark 5) allowing 1–1¼ hours for a large loaf, approximately 45 minutes for small loaves and 20–25 minutes for the cakes. Remove to a wire rack and brush with a wet brush dipped in clear honey or with a sugar glaze whilst still hot.

Bara Brith

Welsh Currant Bread

Makes 2 small loaves

'Bara' means bread and 'Brith' means currants, and this bread is sometimes also known as speckled bread. Nowadays a mixture of dried fruit and a little spice is most frequently added making this a rich spicy fruit bread.

METRIC/IMPERIAL
450 g/1 lb strong white flour
1 teaspoon castor sugar
40 g/1½ oz fresh yeast or 1½ tablespoons dried yeast
175 ml/6 fl oz warm water
1 teaspoon salt
1 teaspoon mixed spice
75 g/3 oz butter, margarine or lard
75 g/3 oz demerara sugar
450 g/1 lb mixed raisins, sultanas, currants and chopped mixed peel
1 standard egg, beaten

Prepare the yeast batter: mix 100 g/4 oz flour, the castor sugar, fresh or dried yeast and warm water together in a large bowl. Cover and set aside until frothy, about

20 minutes in a warm place, longer in a cool one. Mix the remaining flour with the salt and mixed spice, and then rub in the fat until the mixture resembles breadcrumbs. Stir in the sugar and dried fruits. Add the flour mixture and egg to the yeast batter and mix well to form a soft dough, adding extra flour if the dough is too sticky to handle.

Turn the dough onto a lightly floured surface and knead for about 10 minutes by hand or 2–3 minutes using a mixer and dough hook. Shape the dough into a ball and place in an oiled polythene bag and leave to rise until doubled in size, about 2 hours at room temperature and less in a warm place. Turn out onto a lightly floured surface, knock-back and knead for 2 minutes.

Divide into 2 pieces and shape to fit two well greased small (450-g/1-lb) loaf tins. Cover and prove until the dough stands 2·5 cm/1 inch above the top of the tins. Bake in the centre of a moderate oven (180°C., 350°F., Gas Mark 4) for about 50 minutes.

Remove from the tins and place on a wire rack. Brush the tops of the hot loaves with a wet brush dipped in honey or with a sugar glaze.

Irish Barmbrack

Makes 2 small 'bracks'

Similar in appearance to the Welsh Bara Brith, this is the traditional spicy fruit bread of Ireland. It is prepared in the same way as a dough cake by adding the sugar, fat and fruit to the risen dough.

METRIC/IMPERIAL
25 g/1 oz fresh yeast or 3 teaspoons dried yeast
1 teaspoon castor sugar
450 ml/¾ pint warm milk and water mixed
675 g/1½ lb strong white flour
2 teaspoons salt
50 g/2 oz butter or margarine
50 g/2 oz castor sugar
225 g/8 oz sultanas
50 g/2 oz currants
½ teaspoon mixed spice
50 g/2 oz chopped mixed peel

Prepare the dough as for Plain White Bread (Standard Method) (see page 30). Place the knocked-back risen dough in a large bowl and work in the butter or margarine, the sugar, dried fruit, spice and peel by squeezing and kneading until they are evenly mixed through the dough.

Divide the dough into 2 pieces and shape to fit two well greased small (450-g/1-lb) loaf tins. Cover and prove. Brush the tops with milk. Bake in the centre of a moderately hot oven (200°C., 400°F., Gas Mark 6) for 35–40 minutes. Turn out onto a wire rack and cool.
Note A similar bread can be made without yeast (see page 147).

Overleaf *Saffron 'Cake' Bread and Irish Barmbrack*

Selkirk Bannock

This is quite unlike the oatcake bannock since it is a round, flat, yeasted fruit loaf. It was originally made only with sultanas; however nowadays a little candied orange peel is sometimes added.

METRIC/IMPERIAL
450 g/1 lb strong white flour
1 teaspoon castor sugar
15 g/½ oz fresh yeast or 1½ teaspoons dried yeast
250 ml/8 fl oz warm milk
1 teaspoon salt
50 g/2 oz butter or lard
100 g/4 oz castor sugar
225 g/8 oz sultanas
50 g/2 oz chopped candied orange peel (optional)

Prepare the yeast batter: mix 100 g/4 oz flour, 1 teaspoon sugar, the fresh or dried yeast and warm milk together in a large bowl. Cover and set aside until frothy, about 20 minutes in a warm place, longer in a cool one. Mix the remaining flour with the salt and rub in the fat until the mixture resembles breadcrumbs. Add the flour mixture and sugar to the yeast batter and mix well to give a soft dough, adding extra flour if the dough is too sticky to handle.

Turn the dough onto a lightly floured surface and knead until smooth and elastic. It will take about 10 minutes by hand or 2–3 minutes with a mixer and dough hook. Shape the dough into a ball and place in an oiled polythene bag and leave to rise until doubled in size. Put the risen dough into a large bowl, add the sultanas and peel and work into the dough by squeezing and kneading until evenly mixed.

Turn out onto a lightly floured surface and shape into a round, 18 cm/7 inches in diameter. Place on a greased baking tray allowing room at the sides for spreading. Cover and prove for about 1 hour in a warm place. Brush with egg wash or sugar glaze. Bake in the centre of a moderate oven (180°C., 350°F., Gas Mark 4) for about 50 minutes.

Serve hot or cold, cut in slices and buttered.

Scottish Bannocks and Oatcakes

Makes 1 large bannock or 8 small ones

Bannocks or oatcakes are prepared from medium oatmeal and are non-yeasted. They are traditionally baked on a griddle or girdle, however, a heavy frying pan can be used instead, or they can be baked in a moderate oven. They are served with fish or soups or for breakfast. They are best stored in an airtight tin, and either heated in a warm oven or lightly toasted to crisp them before serving.

METRIC/IMPERIAL
275 g/10 oz medium oatmeal
¼ teaspoon salt
¼ teaspoon bicarbonate of soda
25 g/1 oz lard
75 ml/3 fl oz boiling water

Mix the oatmeal with the salt and bicarbonate of soda in a bowl. Melt the lard in the boiling water and add to the dry ingredients. Mix to form a soft dough. Sprinkle the work surface thickly with oatmeal. Turn out the dough and knead well, with the hands covered in oatmeal to prevent sticking, and form into a ball. Press down a little, keeping the edges as round as possible, then roll out to a round 5 mm/¼ inch thick. Trim the edges by putting a dinner plate on top and cutting round it.

Sprinkle with a little more oatmeal and either bake whole or divide into 8. Flour a griddle or baking tray. If baking on a griddle or in a heavy frying pan, warm the griddle or pan first and then put on the oatcake(s), and cook until the edges curl slightly. Crisp the top side under a medium hot grill. If baking in the oven, place on the baking tray and bake towards the top of a moderate oven (160°C., 325°F., Gas Mark 3) for about 30 minutes. Cool on a wire rack.
Note Oatcakes should be lightly coloured and not brown.

Scotch Baps and Morning Rolls

Makes 1 bap and 4 morning rolls or 10 morning rolls

These are the traditional flat yeasted loaves and rolls of Scotland. Small baps are known as morning rolls and were at one time served exclusively at breakfast.

METRIC/IMPERIAL
15 g/½ oz fresh yeast or 1½ teaspoons dried yeast
1 teaspoon castor sugar
300 ml/½ pint warm milk and water mixed
450 g/1 lb strong white flour
1 teaspoon salt
50 g/2 oz lard

Prepare the yeast liquid: blend the fresh yeast in the warm liquid until dissolved or dissolve 1 teaspoon sugar in the warm liquid and sprinkle in the dried yeast. Leave in a warm place for 10 minutes or until dissolved and frothy. Mix the flour and salt together and rub in the lard until the mixture resembles breadcrumbs. Add the yeast liquid to the dry ingredients and mix to form a soft dough, adding extra flour if it is too sticky to handle.

Turn the dough onto a lightly floured surface and knead until smooth and elastic and no longer sticky – about 10 minutes by hand. Shape the dough into a ball and place in an oiled polythene bag and leave to rise until doubled in size. Remove from the polythene bag, knock-back and knead until the dough is firm, about 2 minutes. Shape the dough into rolls or a bap and rolls.

Morning rolls Divide into 10 equal pieces. Shape each piece into a ball and roll out to an oval shape about 7·5 cm/3 inches long, 5 cm/2 inches wide and 1 cm/½ inch thick. Place on a floured baking tray, brush with milk and if liked floury, dust with flour.

Bap and morning rolls Use two-thirds of the dough to make the large bap. Shape it into a ball and roll it out to a round 2 cm/¾ inch thick. Place on a floured baking tray, brush with milk and if liked floury, dust with flour. Divide the remaining third of the dough into 4 and shape as above into rolls.

Cover and prove. Press each morning roll and bap gently in the centre with three fingers to prevent blisters. Bake towards the top of a moderately hot oven (200°C., 400°F., Gas Mark 6) allowing 15–20 minutes for the morning rolls and 20–25 minutes for the bap. Cool on a wire rack.

Aberdeen Buttery Rowies

Makes 15

These are traditional Aberdeen butter yeast rolls, which are similar to croissants in flavour but not in shape.

METRIC / IMPERIAL
550 g / 1¼ lb (½ basic recipe) risen plain white dough (see page 30)
175 g / 6 oz butter
75 g / 3 oz lard

Roll out the risen dough to a rectangle 15 cm/6 inches by 38 cm/15 inches on a lightly floured surface. Cream the butter and lard together and divide into 3 equal portions. Dot one-third of the fat evenly over two-thirds of the dough. Fold the uncovered third of the dough up and the top third down. Seal the edges by pressing with a rolling pin. Give a half turn to the dough and roll out as above again. Repeat this process of rolling and turning twice more.

Roll out again to a rectangle 1 cm/½ inch thick. Cut into small oval shapes 7·5 cm/3 inches by 5 cm/2

inches (or small rounds 6 cm/2½ inches in diameter), or pull off 15 rough lumps from the piece of dough.

Cover and put to rise for 45 minutes in a warm place. Bake towards the top of a moderately hot oven (200°C., 400°F., Gas Mark 6) for about 20 minutes.
Note Always serve Buttery Rowies warm.

Devonshire or Cornish Splits

Makes 14 rolls

These are light yeast rolls, which are served warm cut through and spread with butter or Devonshire or Cornish clotted cream or cold and filled with jam and clotted cream. Occasionally treacle is used instead of jam; this is known as 'thunder and lightning'.

METRIC / IMPERIAL
15 g / ½ oz fresh yeast or 1½ teaspoons dried yeast
1 teaspoon castor sugar
150 ml / ¼ pint warm milk
150 ml / ¼ pint warm water
450 g / 1 lb strong white flour
½ teaspoon salt
25 g / 1 oz butter or margarine

Prepare the dough and rise as for Plain White Bread (Standard Method) (see page 30).

Divide the risen dough into 14 equal pieces and shape into rolls. Place well apart on greased baking trays. Cover and prove until doubled in size.

Brush the rolls with milk or egg wash. Bake towards the top of a hot oven (220°C., 425°F., Gas Mark 7) for 15–20 minutes. Cool on a wire rack.

Overleaf Selkirk Bannock, Scotch Baps, Aberdeen Buttery Rowies and Oatcakes

Kentish Huffkins

Makes 10 cakes

These are plain white, flat yeast cakes with a depression in the centre.

METRIC / IMPERIAL
15 g / ½ oz fresh yeast or 1½ teaspoons dried yeast
1 teaspoon castor sugar
300 ml / ½ pint warm milk and water mixed
450 g / 1 lb strong white flour
½ teaspoon salt
25 g / 1 oz lard

Prepare the dough and rise as for Plain White Bread (Standard Method) (see page 30). Divide the risen dough into 10 equal pieces and shape into flat oval cakes about 1 cm / ½ inch thick. (It is best to do this by forming a roll first and then rolling to an oval shape with a rolling pin.)

Place well apart on greased baking trays and press a floured finger into the centre of each cake. Cover and prove until doubled in size. Bake towards the top of a hot oven (230°C., 450°F., Gas Mark 8) for 15–20 minutes. Transfer to a wire rack and serve hot or cold, split and buttered.

Muffins

Makes 10–12

These are part of our heritage and were sold in the streets by the 'muffin-man' in days gone by. They are cake-like in texture and outwardly resemble the soft roll or floury bap of Scotland and the North of England. They may be cooked on a hot plate, griddle or heavy frying pan or in the oven. To serve, muffins should be pulled open all round the edges with fingers, toasted slowly on both sides, then pulled apart and each piece well buttered. The two halves are put together again and kept warm until eaten.

METRIC / IMPERIAL
15 g / ½ oz fresh yeast or 1½ teaspoons dried yeast
1 teaspoon castor sugar
300 ml / ½ pint warm water
450 g / 1 lb strong white flour
1 teaspoon salt

Prepare the yeast liquid: blend the fresh yeast in the warm water or dissolve the sugar in the warm water and sprinkle in the dried yeast. Allow to stand until frothy, about 10 minutes. Mix the flour and salt together. Add the yeast liquid and mix to form a soft dough. Turn out onto a lightly floured surface and knead until smooth and elastic, about 10 minutes by hand. Shape into a ball and place inside an oiled polythene bag and leave to rise until doubled in size. Remove from the polythene bag, knock-back and knead until the dough is firm, about 2 minutes. Cover and relax for 5 minutes. Roll out onto a floured surface to 1 cm / ½ inch thick. Cover again and relax for a further 5 minutes.

Cut into 9-cm / 3½-inch rounds with a plain cutter. Re-roll and cut rounds from the remains until all the dough is used. Place on a well floured baking tray and dust the tops with flour or fine semolina. Cover and prove until doubled in size, about 15–30 minutes in a warm place.

Heat a griddle, hot plate or heavy frying pan and grease lightly. Cook the muffins for about 3 minutes or until golden brown on each side, or bake towards the top of a hot oven (230°C., 450°F., Gas Mark 8) for about 10 minutes, turning over carefully with a palette knife after 5 minutes. Cool on a wire rack.

Crumpets

Pikelets

Makes 12–15

Crumpets are soft, flat round yeast cakes which have a distinctive honeycomb texture. They are baked on a griddle in a metal ring and because of the action of sudden bottom heat on the yeast and raising agent, gas bubbles are formed quickly and burst at the surface giving the top a pitted appearance. They are served hot, toasted on both sides and well buttered.

Pikelet is the name often used in the North and Midlands of England. (A Scotch crumpet resembles the English crumpet in name only and is another name for a Scotch pancake. A Welsh pikelet is much thinner and usually made without yeast.)

METRIC / IMPERIAL
350 g / 12 oz strong white flour
15 g / ½ oz fresh yeast or 1½ teaspoons dried yeast
350 ml / 12 fl oz warm water
½ teaspoon bicarbonate of soda
2 teaspoons salt
150 ml / ¼ pint warm milk

Blend the flour, fresh or dried yeast and warm water together in a large mixing bowl. Cover with a sheet of oiled polythene and set aside until very light and frothy, about 1 hour in a warm place. Add the bicarbonate of soda and salt to the warm milk and stir into the batter, adding a little extra milk if necessary to give a runny batter. Cover again and stand until frothy, for about 30 minutes to 1 hour in a warm place.

Heat a griddle or heavy frying pan and very lightly grease the surface. Grease the crumpet rings, or 7·5–9-cm / 3–3½-inch plain pastry cutters or poaching rings will do. Place the rings on the hot griddle or frying pan. Pour about 2 tablespoons of the mixture into each ring. Turn down the heat and cook gently for about 10 minutes or until the crumpets are well set and the bubbles have burst. Remove the rings, turn the crumpets over and cook for a further 2–3 minutes until they are a pale golden brown and thoroughly dried. Repeat until all the mixture has been used up.

Manchets

Manche means hand bread. These were laid for each person on the tables of noble men in mediaeval times. They were prepared from fine white sifted flour which in those times was available only to the nobility; the servants and peasants were left to eat the bread prepared from the bran. The dough was divided into individual pieces, formed into an oval shape then cut on the top with a knife to give it room to rise.

METRIC/IMPERIAL
350 g / 12 oz risen plain white dough (see page 30)
milk to glaze

Divide the dough into 4 (75-g / 3-oz) pieces. Knead and shape each piece into an oval shape. Place on a greased and floured baking tray and make diagonal cuts across the tops with a sharp knife. Brush the tops with milk, cover and prove. Bake towards the top of a hot oven (230°C., 450°F., Gas Mark 8) for 15–20 minutes. Cool on a wire rack.

St. Albans Pope Ladies

Makes 12

This recipe is a modern adaptation of a traditional New Year's bread said to originate in St. Albans. The Pope Ladies are said to be named after the mythical Popess Joan of 858 AD.

METRIC/IMPERIAL
850 g / 1 lb 14 oz risen sweet bread dough
(see page 35)
24 currants

Divide the dough into 12 equal pieces. (Each piece will form 1 Pope Lady.) Cut each piece of dough in half. To form the body, shape a 7·5-cm/3-inch oval from one half. Use a little more than half of the remaining dough to form the head. Shape it into a round ball. Press 2 currants in deeply for the eyes and put a tiny piece of dough on for the nose. Use the remaining dough for the arms by making a 10-cm/4-inch long roll and cutting it into 2 pieces. Assemble these pieces in the shape of ladies, placing well apart on greased baking trays. Cover and prove for about 30 minutes in a warm place. Brush with egg wash. Bake towards the top of a moderately hot oven (190°C., 375°F., Gas Mark 5) for 15–20 minutes. Serve warm with butter.

Yorkshire Teacakes

Makes 6

Traditional tea time fare on all Yorkshire tables, these yeasted teacakes have become popular all over the country. They are thought to be direct descendants of manchet bread. They may be plain or fruited but are always served hot, split and buttered or toasted and buttered. The way to butter toasted teacakes so that the butter is evenly distributed (and does not all soak down into the bottom crust) is to toast the bottoms and tops first, then split and toast the insides. Cover the bottom half with pats of butter (do not spread), replace top half and invert. Keep hot for 2–3 minutes, then turn right side up, cut in quarters and serve.

METRIC/IMPERIAL
15 g / ½ oz fresh yeast or 1½ teaspoons dried yeast
1 teaspoon castor sugar
300 ml / ½ pint warm milk or milk and water
450 g / 1 lb strong white flour
1 teaspoon salt
50 g / 2 oz lard or butter
25 g / 1 oz castor sugar
50 g / 2 oz currants (optional)
25 g / 1 oz chopped mixed peel (optional)

Prepare the yeast liquid: blend the fresh yeast in the warm liquid until dissolved or dissolve 1 teaspoon sugar in the warm liquid and sprinkle in the dried yeast. Leave in a warm place for about 10 minutes or until dissolved and frothy.

Mix the flour and salt together and rub in the fat until the mixture resembles breadcrumbs. Stir in the sugar and fruits, if used. Add the yeast liquid to the dry ingredients and mix to form a soft dough, adding extra flour if it is too sticky to handle.

Turn the dough onto a lightly floured surface and knead until smooth and elastic. It will take about 10 minutes by hand or 2–3 minutes with a mixer and dough hook. Place the dough inside an oiled polythene bag and leave to rise until doubled in size, about 1½ hours at room temperature, less in a warm place. Remove from the polythene bag, knock-back and knead until the dough is firm, about 2 minutes.

Divide into 6 equal pieces and shape into balls. Roll each out to a flattened round, 12·5–15 cm/5–6 inches in diameter. Place on greased baking trays and brush the tops with milk. Cover and prove. Bake just above the centre of a moderately hot oven (200°C., 400°F., Gas Mark 6) for about 20 minutes.

Turn onto a wire rack and cover with a tea towel before cooling or rub the tops of the teacakes lightly with butter or margarine whilst still hot to keep the crust soft. Serve hot or toasted, buttered liberally.

Overleaf Kentish Huffkins (see page 78), Sally Lunn (page 82) and Crumpets (page 78)

Sally Lunns

Makes 2

These are round bun-type cakes, said to be 'flat golden on top and flat white below'. They are said by some people to be called after a buxom Sally Lunn who lived in Bath; however, there are many more stories regarding the origin of the name of this bun. Traditionally the buns were made in special Sally Lunn rings, but a small round cake tin can be substituted. Also traditionally they were split hot and embosomed in clouds of whipped cream and strewn with crushed sugar; nowadays they are more often buttered or filled with clotted cream.

METRIC/IMPERIAL
50 g/2 oz butter
300 ml/½ pint milk
1 teaspoon castor sugar
15 g/½ oz fresh yeast or 1½ teaspoons dried yeast
2 standard eggs
450 g/1 lb strong white flour
1 teaspoon salt

Melt the butter slowly in a pan, remove from heat and add the milk and sugar. Add the fresh or dried yeast to the warm milk mixture. If using fresh yeast blend well and use right away, but if using dried yeast leave to stand for about 10 minutes or until frothy.

Beat the eggs and add with the flour and salt to the yeast liquid. Mix well to form a soft dough. (The dough will be too soft to knead.) Beat for 2–3 minutes, then pour into two greased 12·5-cm/5-inch or 15-cm/6-inch round cake tins. Cover with an oiled polythene bag or sheet and prove until the mixture has doubled in size and is nearly to the top of the tins, about 1½ hours in a warm place. Bake in the centre of a hot oven (220°C., 425°F., Gas Mark 7) for 20–25 minutes. Turn out onto a wire rack and brush the tops with a sugar glaze whilst still hot.

Hot Cross Buns

Makes 12

These spicy yeast buns are traditionally served for breakfast on Good Friday. As the name implies they have a cross on top. In fact spice and the cross are essential in all hot cross buns. The cross may be made in one of the following ways:
(1) by cutting a cross on top of the shaped buns with a sharp knife before proving;
(2) by using small strips of pastry (may be trimmings) to form a cross on the risen buns. The pastry is sometimes removed after baking, leaving behind the outline of the cross;
(3) by using strips of candied peel on the risen buns, which is left on and eaten after baking;
(4) by piping a flour and water paste cross on the risen buns before baking.

METRIC/IMPERIAL
450 g/1 lb strong white flour
25 g/1 oz fresh yeast or 3 teaspoons dried yeast
1 teaspoon castor sugar
150 ml/¼ pint warm milk
75 ml/3 fl oz warm water
1 teaspoon salt
½ teaspoon mixed spice
½ teaspoon ground cinnamon
½ teaspoon grated nutmeg
50 g/2 oz castor sugar
50 g/2 oz butter, softened
1 standard egg, beaten
100 g/4 oz currants
50 g/2 oz chopped mixed peel

Prepare the yeast batter: mix 100 g/4 oz flour, 1 teaspoon sugar, the fresh or dried yeast and the warm milk and water together in a large bowl. Cover and set aside until frothy, about 20 minutes in a warm place, longer in a cool one.

Mix the remaining flour with the salt, spices and sugar. Add the dry ingredients, softened butter, beaten egg, currants and mixed peel to the yeast batter and mix well to form a soft dough, adding extra flour if the dough is too sticky to handle.

Turn the dough onto a lightly floured surface and knead until smooth, about 10 minutes by hand or 2–3 minutes with a mixer and dough hook. Shape the dough into a ball and place inside an oiled polythene bag and leave to rise until doubled in size, about 2 hours at room temperature, less in a warm place. Turn out onto a lightly floured surface, knock-back and knead for 2 minutes.

Divide the dough into 12 equal pieces and shape into buns. Place well apart on greased baking trays. Cover and put to rise for about 30 minutes in a warm place until doubled in size. Make a cross on each bun (see opposite). Bake just above the centre of a moderately hot oven (190°C., 375°F., Gas Mark 5) for 15–20 minutes. Remove to a wire rack and brush the hot buns with a sugar glaze.

London Buns

Makes 12

The traditional recipe for London Buns contained currants, powdered nutmeg and caraway seeds and they were oval in shape.

METRIC/IMPERIAL
450 g/1 lb strong white flour
1 teaspoon castor sugar
25 g/1 oz fresh yeast or 3 teaspoons dried yeast
225 ml/7 fl oz warm milk and water mixed
1 teaspoon salt
50 g/2 oz butter or margarine
50 g/2 oz castor sugar
100 g/4 oz currants
½ teaspoon caraway seeds (optional)
½ teaspoon ground nutmeg

Prepare and rise the dough as for Sweet Bread (Standard Method) (see page 35) adding the currants, caraway seeds (if used) and nutmeg to the dry ingredients. Divide the risen and knocked-back dough into 12 equal pieces. Shape each piece into an oval bun and place well apart on greased baking trays.

Cover and prove until doubled in size. Bake towards the top of a moderately hot oven (190°C., 375°F., Gas Mark 5) for 15–20 minutes. Remove to a wire rack and brush the hot buns with a wet brush dipped in honey or with a sugar glaze. Leave to get cold.

Overleaf *Hot Cross Buns*

83

Chelsea Buns

Makes 9

Originally made in the Old Chelsea Bun House in Pimlico Road, these buns were so popular that as many as a quarter of a million were sold in a day.

METRIC/IMPERIAL
225 g/8 oz strong white flour
½ teaspoon castor sugar
15 g/½ oz fresh yeast or 1½ teaspoons dried yeast
75 ml/3 fl oz warm milk
½ teaspoon salt
15 g/½ oz butter, margarine or lard
1 standard egg, beaten
FILLING
15 g/½ oz butter or margarine, melted
75 g/3 oz mixed currants, sultanas and raisins
25 g/1 oz chopped mixed peel
50 g/2 oz soft brown sugar

Prepare the yeast batter: mix 50 g/2 oz flour, ½ teaspoon sugar, the fresh or dried yeast and warm milk together in a bowl. Cover and set aside until frothy, about 20 minutes in a warm place, longer in a cool one. Mix the remaining flour with the salt and rub in the fat until the mixture resembles fine breadcrumbs. Add the egg with the flour mixture to the yeast batter and mix well to give a soft dough, adding extra flour if the dough is too sticky to handle.

Turn the dough onto a lightly floured surface and knead until smooth and elastic, about 5–10 minutes. Shape the dough into a ball, place inside an oiled polythene bag and leave to rise until doubled in size. Turn the risen dough onto a lightly floured surface, knock-back and knead until the dough is firm, about 1–2 minutes.

Roll the dough out to a rectangle 30 cm/12 inches by 23 cm/9 inches and brush with melted butter or margarine. Mix the dried fruit, mixed peel and brown sugar together and sprinkle evenly over the dough. Roll up from the long edge to give a 30-cm/12-inch roll. Cut into 9 equal slices and place these, cut face down, well apart on a lightly greased baking tray or in an 18-cm/7-inch square baking tin in three rows of three. Cover and prove until doubled in size, about 30 minutes in a warm place.

Bake just above the centre of a moderately hot oven (190°C., 375°F., Gas Mark 5) for 15–20 minutes on a baking tray or for 20–25 minutes in a tin. Brush the tops of the hot buns with a wet brush dipped in honey or with a sugar glaze. Cool on a wire rack.
Note To serve the buns baked in a tin, pull apart first.

Bath Buns

Makes 12

These are made from a rich, soft, sticky dough which results in their uneven shape, since they cannot be shaped by hand. Traditionally finished with crushed lump sugar.

METRIC / IMPERIAL
450 g / 1 lb strong white flour
1 teaspoon castor sugar
25 g / 1 oz fresh yeast or 3 teaspoons dried yeast
200 ml / 7 fl oz warm milk and water mixed
1 teaspoon salt
50 g / 2 oz butter or margarine
75 g / 3 oz castor sugar
2 standard eggs, beaten
100 g / 4 oz sultanas
25–50 g / 1–2 oz chopped mixed peel
FINISH
50 g / 2 oz lump sugar or sugar nibs

Prepare the yeast batter: mix 100 g / 4 oz flour, 1 teaspoon sugar, the fresh or dried yeast and warm liquid together in a large bowl. Cover and set aside until frothy, about 20 minutes in a warm place, longer in a cool one. Mix the remaining flour with the salt, rub in the fat until the mixture resembles breadcrumbs, and stir in the sugar. Add the eggs, the dry ingredients, sultanas and mixed peel to the yeast batter and mix well to give a soft dough.

(The dough will be too sticky to knead by hand, but there is no need to add more flour.)

Leave the dough in the bowl and beat with a wooden spoon, one hand or use a dough hook and mixer, until the gluten is developed, about 10 minutes by hand or 2 minutes using a mixer. Cover the bowl and leave to rise until doubled in size, about 1–1½ hours in a warm place. Beat the risen dough for 2 minutes then place tablespoons of the dough well apart on greased baking trays.

Cover and prove. Brush with egg wash and sprinkle the coarsely crushed lump sugar or sugar nibs over the tops of the buns. Bake towards the top of a moderately hot oven (190°C., 375°F., Gas Mark 5) for 15–20 minutes. Cool on a wire rack.

Chapter 6

Breads from Many Countries

Breads from many countries make a fascinating study. Even today, one can still follow some of the old trade routes by tracing on the map similar breads eaten in different countries in different parts of the world. Some countries, no longer part of an empire, still eat the breads of the former empire while other countries, now themselves belonging to 20th century empires, still maintain their individuality with their daily bread.

Although there is a wide variety of breads included in this chapter it is limited by the availability in some places of necessary ingredients. Also some breads are so personal to their country of origin that they might be unpalatable to us. The fascinating Ethiopian 'Injerra', almost like foam rubber by itself but delicious eaten with the peppery food of the country, could not

be included for this reason. The other point worth remembering is that breads prepared in their country of origin always taste better there than they do when prepared elsewhere in a different climate and with different accompanying tastes (and smells!). It is difficult to decide if this difference is due to the slight variance of ingredients or the evocative memories the breads hold!

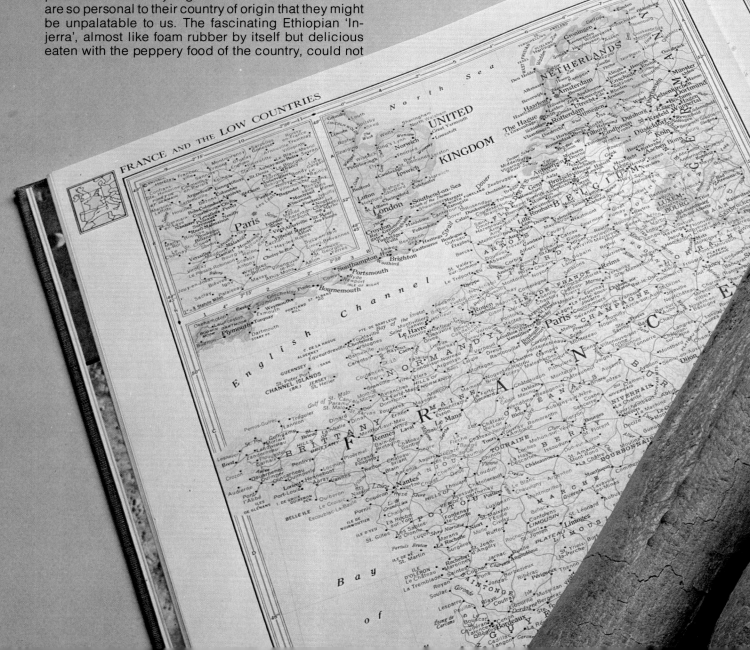

Austrian Hausbrot with Potatoes

A particularly delicious moist bread – ideal to serve instead of potatoes with hot flavoursome beef casseroles.

METRIC/IMPERIAL
175 g/6 oz even-sized potatoes
300 ml/½ pint warm water
15 g/½ oz fresh yeast or 1½ teaspoons dried yeast
1 teaspoon sugar
1½ teaspoons salt
1 teaspoon fennel powder or caraway seeds
350 g/12 oz rye flour
350 g/12 oz wholewheat flour

Cook the potatoes in their skins until tender, then drain well. Peel and press the cooked potatoes through a sieve; then mix into all but 4 tablespoons of the warm water.

(The peeled potatoes may be liquidised with the water.)

Mix the yeast into the remaining warm water, blending it well. Then add 1 teaspoon sugar and place aside for about 10 minutes. Stir the salt and the fennel or caraway seeds into the lukewarm potato mixture then work in the dissolved yeast, the rye flour and the wholewheat flour to make a firm dough. Turn the dough out onto a lightly floured surface and knead well until smooth, then shape into a ball and place in an oiled polythene bag. Put to rise in a warm place until it has risen to almost double in size. Remove the dough from the bag and knock-back. Shape into a round loaf and place on a greased baking tray. Put the loaf aside in a cool place so that it rises very slowly – preferably overnight.

Bake the bread towards the top of a moderately hot oven (200°C., 400°F., Gas Mark 6) for 35–45 minutes, brushing the top of the loaf with water from time to time during cooking. When the loaf is well risen, browned on the top and sounds hollow when tapped on the base it is cooked. Cool on a wire rack.

Vienna Bread

Makes 5 loaves

Crisp-crusted Vienna loaves.

METRIC/IMPERIAL
40 g/1½ oz fresh yeast or 5 teaspoons dried yeast
450 ml/¾ pint lukewarm water and milk mixed
1 teaspoon castor sugar
25 g/1 oz lard
675 g/1½ lb strong white flour
2 teaspoons salt
creamy milk for glazing

Stir the yeast into the lukewarm milk and water mixture with the sugar until well blended. Leave aside for 5–10 minutes until frothy. Rub the lard into the flour and salt in a large bowl. Stir in the yeast liquid and mix to a firm dough, adding a little extra flour if it is too sticky to handle. Work with your hand until the dough is evenly blended then turn the dough out onto a lightly floured surface and knead thoroughly until firm, elastic and no longer sticky. This will take about 10 minutes.

Shape the dough into a ball and place in a large oiled polythene bag loosely tied at the top. Leave to rise at room temperature until the dough has doubled in size. Turn risen dough onto a lightly floured surface, knock-back and knead until smooth. Divide the dough into 5 equal pieces weighing about 225 g/8 oz each. Roll out each piece to an oval about 23 cm/9 inches in length and roll each piece up from the long side to form a tight roll. Place the Vienna loaves on lightly greased baking trays with the seam underneath and leave to rise until doubled in size.

Prepare a hot oven (230°C., 450°F., Gas Mark 8) in which two tins of water have been placed in the bottom to produce a steamy atmosphere. Make 4 diagonal cuts across each of the loaves with a sharp knife then bake them towards the top of the oven for about 15 minutes. Open the oven door, remove the tins of water and let the steam escape, then brush the loaves with creamy milk and bake for a further 5–10 minutes without the steam to give the desired crispy crust. Cool on a wire rack.

Note Vienna rolls may also be made from the same dough using about 50 g/2 oz dough per roll, yielding about 20 rolls.

Viennese Striezel

Attractively plaited sweet fruit bread.

METRIC/IMPERIAL
25 g/1 oz fresh yeast or 3 teaspoons dried yeast
225 ml/7½ fl oz warm milk
75 g/3 oz castor sugar
500 g/1 lb 2 oz strong white flour
¼ teaspoon salt
100 g/4 oz butter, melted
2 eggs
100 g/4 oz raisins
grated rind of 1 lemon
TOPPING
few split blanched almonds and sugar crystals
(optional)

Stir the yeast into the warm milk with 1 teaspoon of the sugar until well blended. Leave aside for 5–10 minutes until frothy. Combine the flour and salt and add the yeast liquid, the remaining sugar and the melted butter. Separate 1 of the eggs and add the egg yolk and the other egg to the mixture. Beat the egg white lightly and reserve. Mix the rest of the ingredients together to give a soft but not sticky dough. Turn onto a lightly floured surface and knead the mixture well. Then knead in the raisins and grated lemon rind until evenly mixed.

Divide the dough as follows: 4 equal fairly thick balls; 3 equal balls half the size of the first balls; and 2 smaller still. Roll out all the pieces of dough to strands about the same length (33 cm / 13 inches). Plait the first 4 thickest strands together (for plaiting 4 strands see instruction on page 115); then plait the next 3 strands together. Twist the remaining 2 smaller strands together. Place the largest plait on a greased baking tray. Brush it with the reserved beaten egg white then place the 3-roll plait in the centre on top, brush with egg white and then finally position the twisted strips on top. Brush the whole loaf with egg white and if liked strew the top with split blanched almonds and sugar crystals. Place the Striezel aside in a warm place for about 1 hour until it is well risen.

Bake in the centre of a hot oven (230°C., 450°F., Gas Mark 8) for about 20 minutes until the loaf is golden brown on top. Then reduce the temperature to moderate (180°C., 350°F., Gas Mark 4) and continue baking for a further 35 minutes. Cool on a wire rack.

Coûque de Visé

A sugar-crusted sweet Belgian brioche.

METRIC / IMPERIAL
15 g / ½ oz fresh yeast or 1½ teaspoons dried yeast
2 tablespoons lukewarm water
3 teaspoons castor sugar
6 tablespoons milk
100 g / 4 oz butter or margarine
½ teaspoon salt
350 g / 12 oz strong white flour
2 large eggs, beaten
5 tablespoons coarse coffee sugar crystals
egg yolk

Stir the yeast into the lukewarm water with ½ teaspoon of the castor sugar until it is well blended; leave aside for 5–10 minutes until frothy. Bring the milk to the boil, add the butter or margarine, the remaining castor sugar and the salt; stir until dissolved, then leave aside to cool until lukewarm. Measure about 200 g / 7 oz of the flour into a large bowl and mix in the beaten eggs with the yeast liquid and milk mixture; beat well so that the mixture is smooth then work in the remaining flour to give a fairly soft dough. Turn the dough out onto a lightly floured surface and knead well until smooth and satiny. Shape the dough into a ball and place in an oiled polythene bag. Leave aside in a warm place until it has doubled in size.

Turn the risen dough out onto a lightly floured surface, knock-back and knead well for a few minutes; then knead in 3 tablespoons of the sugar crystals. Shape the dough into a rectangle. Return the dough to the polythene bag and leave overnight in a refrigerator or cold place. The next morning bring the dough out and let it warm to room temperature. Cut off a piece of the dough the size of an egg. Form the remaining dough into a ball and put it in a greased 1-litre / 2-pint brioche tin or mould. Cut a small cross in the top of the dough and form the remaining small piece of dough into a pear shape. Then insert the point of the pear into the middle of the cross. Leave the dough to rise again in a warm place for about 2 hours or until it has reached the top of the tin. Brush the risen dough with an egg wash made by lightly mixing together the egg yolk with 1 teaspoon of water, then sprinkle with the remaining 2 tablespoons sugar crystals.

Bake in the centre of a moderately hot oven (190°C., 375°F., Gas Mark 5) for about 40 minutes. If the bread looks as if the top might overbrown during cooking, cover it with a small piece of foil. When the base of the brioche is tapped and it sounds hollow it is ready. Turn it out onto a wire rack and leave to cool.

Pãezinhos de Batata Doce

Brazilian Sweet Potato Rolls

Makes 24 rolls or 12 rolls and 1 small loaf

Although the recipe uses sweet potatoes it is equally good made with ordinary potatoes.

METRIC / IMPERIAL
350 g / 12 oz strong white flour
50 g / 2 oz maize meal
350 g / 12 oz sweet or ordinary potatoes
50 g / 2 oz butter or margarine
1 teaspoon salt
15 g / ½ oz fresh yeast or 1½ teaspoons dried yeast
100 ml / 4 fl oz warm milk
1½ teaspoons castor sugar
2 eggs, lightly beaten
½ teaspoon aniseed seeds (optional)

Sift the flour and maize meal together. Peel and cook the potatoes in salted water until tender. Drain and mash smoothly then beat in the butter and salt. Leave until lukewarm. Meanwhile whisk the yeast into the warm milk; add the sugar, the lightly beaten eggs and the aniseed and mix well. Add about 100 g / 4 oz of the flour and maize meal mixture to make a batter. Cover with a plate and leave aside in a warm place for about 30 minutes until it is spongy; then mix it into the warm potatoes. Gradually work more of the flour and maize meal into the potato mixture until you have added sufficient flour to give a workable dough.

Turn the dough out onto a lightly floured surface and knead it with any remaining flour until it is no longer sticky. It may be necessary to add a little extra flour. Place the dough in a greased polythene bag and put aside in a warm place until it has doubled in size. Break the dough into 72 pieces and shape into small balls about the size of a walnut (or 36 balls using half of the dough). Place groups of 3 balls into greased patty tins. Cover the tins loosely with greased polythene and put in a warm place until doubled in size.

If using half the dough for a loaf, shape it and place in a greased small (450-g / 1-lb) loaf tin.

Brush the risen rolls and loaf with beaten egg. Bake towards the top of a moderately hot oven (190°C., 375°F., Gas Mark 5) for about 20 minutes.

91

Bulgarian Boiled Bread Rolls

Makes 30

Small moist rolls with a very crisp crust.

METRIC/IMPERIAL
15 g/½ oz fresh yeast or 1½ teaspoons dried yeast
150 ml/¼ pint warm water
1 teaspoon castor sugar
550 g/1¼ lb strong white flour
½ teaspoon salt
300 ml/½ pint lukewarm milk
15 g/½ oz butter, melted

Stir the yeast into the warm water with the sugar until well blended. Leave aside for 5–10 minutes. Place all the ingredients together with the yeast liquid in a bowl. Mix well, knead thoroughly until smooth and then shape the dough into a ball and place in an oiled polythene bag. Leave aside in a warm place until doubled in size. Divide and form the dough into 30 pieces about the size and shape of a ping-pong ball.

Bring a large saucepan three-quarters full of water to a boil. Reduce the heat so that the water is just simmering then add the yeast balls a few at a time. As soon as they rise to the surface and begin to float, take them out with a slotted spoon and place them in a colander so that any liquid can drain out. Arrange the yeast balls on greased baking trays and slit the top of each with a sharp knife. Leave aside to rise a little.

Bake the rolls towards the top of a hot oven (220°C., 425°F., Gas Mark 7) for about 15 minutes. If they appear to be overbrowning before they are cooked through, cover with a piece of damp greaseproof paper. Cool on a wire rack.

Cheese Pitka

Makes 6 flat or 12 round rolls

Bulgarian softbread rolls with a cheese filling.

METRIC/IMPERIAL
450 g/1 lb strong white flour
½ teaspoon castor sugar
150 ml/¼ pint warm water
2 teaspoons dried yeast
150 ml/¼ pint hot water
1½ teaspoons salt
50–75 g/2–3 oz soft butter
225 g/8 oz Feta or cottage cheese
1 egg, beaten

Measure 25 g/1 oz of the flour and the sugar into a bowl. Add the warm water and the dried yeast and mix well. In another bowl whisk 25 g/1 oz of the flour into the hot water (just off the boil) to make a thick sauce. Cool until lukewarm and then mix it with the yeast liquid and leave aside for about 15 minutes until frothy.

Knead in the remaining flour and the salt to give a firm dough. Knead well. Place the dough in a greased bowl, cover with oiled polythene and leave to rise in a warm place until doubled in size.

Roll out the dough on a floured surface to a rectangle approximately 30 cm/12 inches by 45 cm/18 inches. Spread the dough evenly with the butter and then cut it into 15-cm/6-inch squares. Mix the Feta or cottage cheese with half the beaten egg and place a spoonful in the middle of each square. Fold over the four corners of the square to a point in the centre and place on a greased baking tray. Brush the Pitka with the remaining beaten egg. Bake towards the top of a hot oven (230°C., 450°F., Gas Mark 8) for 10–15 minutes. Cool on a wire rack.

Note This same dough can also be made into plain rolls. Divide into 12 equal pieces, roll into balls, flatten, place on baking sheets and then prick all over. Brush with beaten egg before baking.

Czechoslovakian Rolled Ham Loaf

This rolled ham bread is at its best served hot either with soup or with a side dish of spiced cabbage or sauerkraut.

METRIC/IMPERIAL
450 g/1 lb strong white flour
1 teaspoon salt
300 ml/½ pint water or milk
½ teaspoon sugar
15 g/½ oz fresh yeast or 1½ teaspoons dried yeast
100 g/4 oz onion, finely chopped
½–1 teaspoon mixed dried herbs or 1 teaspoon chopped fresh herbs
¼ teaspoon ground cinnamon
a little grated nutmeg
225 g/8 oz cooked ham (cut into 4 slices)
beaten egg to glaze

Sift the flour and salt in a bowl and leave in a warm place. Heat the water or milk and sugar until it is lukewarm then add the yeast and stir until well blended. Leave aside for about 10 minutes until frothy. Make a well in the centre of the warm flour, add the yeast liquid and mix to a dough. Knead in the bowl until the dough comes away cleanly from the sides. Turn the dough onto a floured surface and knead well for about 10 minutes until smooth. Shape into a ball, place in an oiled polythene bag in a warm place and leave until the dough has doubled in size. Remove the dough from the bag, knock-back and roll out to a rectangle about 20 cm/8 inches by 35 cm/14 inches or the most suitable size for the slices of ham to cover.

Brush the dough with water then sprinkle with the finely chopped onion, the herbs, cinnamon and nutmeg; cover with the slices of ham. Roll the dough up like a Swiss roll, place it on a greased baking tray and brush with beaten egg. Cover and prove.

Bake the loaf just above the centre of a hot oven (220°C., 425°F., Gas Mark 7) for 15 minutes then reduce the temperature to moderately hot (190°C., 375°F., Gas Mark 5) and continue to bake for a further 40 minutes or until the loaf sounds hollow when it is tapped on the base. Cool on a wire rack.

Czechoslovakian Rye Bread

A beery-smelling, rich flavoured bread, worth the time and effort.

METRIC/IMPERIAL
150 g/5 oz sour dough*
300 ml/½ pint warm water
1 teaspoon castor sugar
300 g/11 oz and 2 teaspoons fine rye flour
200 g/7 oz coarse rye meal
1 tablespoon salt
1 tablespoon treacle or sugar
1–2 tablespoons caraway seeds (optional)
2 teaspoons cornflour

*The sour dough can be made by putting aside 150 g/5 oz of any bread dough and leaving it for 3–4 · days – or it may be made as described below.

*INGREDIENTS FOR STARTER DOUGH
METRIC/IMPERIAL
1 tablespoon milk
2 tablespoons water
½ teaspoon vegetable oil
½ teaspoon dried yeast
1 tablespoon warm boiled water
½ teaspoon castor sugar
½ teaspoon salt
75 g/3 oz strong white flour

If not already made, prepare the starter dough: combine the milk, water and oil in a saucepan, bring to the boil then leave aside to cool until lukewarm. Stir the yeast into the warm boiled water with the sugar. Place aside for about 10 minutes until it is beginning to froth, then add it with the salt to the lukewarm milk mixture. Stir this liquid into the flour and blend thoroughly. Leave to stand uncovered at room temperature for 3–5 days. Stir 2–3 times daily and cover at night.

A starter dough should have a yeasty but not a sour smell. Sometimes liquid will come to the top – just stir this back in. When ready turn the starter dough into a polythene box and store in the refrigerator until required to make the bread.

Mash the soured starter dough in a bowl with 4 tablespoons of the warm water then mix in 1 teaspoon sugar and 2 teaspoons of the fine rye flour. Cover and leave in a warm place overnight or for a minimum of 10 hours to ferment. The next morning combine 150 g/5 oz coarse rye meal with a further 100 g/4 oz fine rye flour and 150 ml/¼ pint warm water. Mix this into the ferment, cover and leave in a warm place for 10 hours.

Now add to the mixture that has stood for a total of at least 20 hours, 200 g/7 oz fine rye flour, 50 g/2 oz coarse rye meal, 3 tablespoons warm water, the salt, the treacle or sugar and caraway seeds. Mix well together and then turn out onto an oiled surface and knead well. Shape into a ball, place in an oiled polythene bag and leave aside in a warm place overnight or for a minimum of 10 hours. In the morning shape the dough into a cob, place on a greased baking tray, brush the top with water and then cover with oiled polythene. Stand in a warm place for about 1 hour or until the dough has risen and feels springy when lightly pressed with the finger. Brush the loaf with a starch glaze made by creaming 2 teaspoons cornflour with 2 teaspoons cold water in a cup, and stirring in sufficient boiling water to thicken and clear the mixture.

Bake towards the top of a hot oven (220°C., 425°F., Gas Mark 7) for 30 minutes. Brush with the glaze again, reduce the temperature to moderate (180°C., 350°F., Gas Mark 4), transfer to the centre shelf and continue baking for about 20 minutes or until the base sounds hollow when tapped. Wrap the hot loaf in a clean tea towel and place on a wire rack to cool.

While everyone else calls this light flaky dough Danish pastry, the Danes themselves call it Vienna bread.

About a hundred years ago Danish bakers were paid for their work with board and lodgings. At one point they demanded payment in cash instead, and when this was not forthcoming they went on strike. Their employers sacked them and brought in bakers from Vienna to do the work instead. These Viennese bakers introduced the Danes to their special light flaky dough 'Wienerbrød' that had butter folded in it, and this became very popular. When eventually the problems of the Danish bakers were resolved they returned to work and continued to make the popular Wienerbrød – but not to be outdone they added their own improvements, giving the bread different fillings and toppings to make it even more delicious. The fame of these delicious pastries was spread far and wide and they were known as Danish pastries.

In Denmark the pastries are not only eaten with coffee but as a dessert as well; it is insisted that they be eaten fresh daily, and to ensure this most Danish bakeries open seven days a week.

Dansk Wienerbrød

Danish Pastries

Makes 16 assorted pastries

*This recipe is easier than some and yet the pastries are
particularly good, light and very flaky.
Serve with coffee or hot chocolate.*

METRIC/IMPERIAL
15 g/½ oz fresh yeast or 2 teaspoons dried yeast
6 tablespoons lukewarm water
40 g/1½ oz castor sugar
275 g/10 oz plain flour
¼ teaspoon salt
25 g/1 oz lard
1 large egg
½ teaspoon vanilla essence
175 g/6 oz butter (in one rectangular piece)

Mix the yeast into the lukewarm water with ½ teaspoon
of the castor sugar. Stir until the yeast is well blended
then leave aside for 5–10 minutes until frothy. Place the
flour and salt in a bowl and rub in the lard until the
mixture resembles breadcrumbs. Beat the egg with the
vanilla essence and the remaining castor sugar, add
this with the yeast liquid to the flour and mix together to
give a fairly stiff dough. Turn the dough onto a lightly
floured surface and knead for 5–10 minutes until it is
smooth and elastic. Place the dough in an oiled
polythene bag and place in a refrigerator or a cold
place for 15 minutes to rest.

Take the butter, which should be only just soft
enough to be able to cut it in fairly thin slices, and cut
into about 8 slices 5 mm/¼ inch thick; arrange them on
a plate and place in a refrigerator so they do not soften.
Roll the relaxed dough out to a rectangle about
20 cm/8 inches by 38 cm/15 inches. Place it
lengthwise and arrange 4 of the butter slices in the
centre (see Diagram A). Fold the left-hand half of the
dough over the butter, sealing down all the edges (see
Diagram B). Arrange the remaining butter slices on top
of the folded dough and then fold over the right-hand
side on top, sealing down the edges (see Diagram C).
Roll the folded dough to a rectangle about 40 cm/16
inches by 15 cm/6 inches. Place it lengthwise and fold
both the ends into the centre (a) and then one half on
top of the other to make 4 layers of dough (b) as in
Diagram D. Place the folded dough in the oiled
polythene bag and place in the refrigerator or a cold
place for about 30 minutes.

Again roll the rested dough to a rectangle 40 cm/16
inches by 15 cm/6 inches and repeat the folding as
illustrated in Diagram D then rest the dough in a cool
place for a further 30 minutes. Finally roll and fold
dough into 4 layers once more then wrap and rest for at
least 2 hours (overnight is best) before use. While the
dough is resting select and prepare the fillings. This
recipe shows you how to roll the dough to make 8
different types of Danish pastry, but if you prefer to
make only one or two varieties make the fillings and roll
the dough accordingly.

Fillings for Danish pastries

Almond paste This will fill 12–16 pastries. (For this
pastry recipe make one-third, using ½ a small egg.)
Mix 75 g/3 oz ground almonds with 1 large egg, 4
tablespoons castor sugar and 4 drops almond
essence.

Vanilla cream This will fill 12 pastries. (For this pastry
recipe make one-third, using ½ a small egg.)
Mix 1 egg in a saucepan with 4 teaspoons castor sugar
and 3 teaspoons flour to make a smooth paste; then
blend in 150 ml/¼ pint milk, stir briskly over a low heat
and bring to the boil to make a thick smooth sauce,
then flavour with ½ teaspoon vanilla essence.

Cinnamon sugar This will fill 10 pastries. (For this
pastry recipe make one-quarter.)
Cream together 50 g/2 oz of butter and castor sugar
and 2 teaspoons ground cinnamon.

Apple and raisin This will fill 6–8 pastries. (For this
pastry recipe make one-third.)
Combine 1 peeled and grated cooking apple with 3
tablespoons demerara sugar, 15 g/½ oz butter and a
little grated orange rind or chopped mixed peel.

Ginger Allow 1 globe of stem ginger for 2 pastries. Use
chopped stem ginger and a little of the syrup or ginger
marmalade.

Shaping the pastries
Divide the rested dough in half and roll one half to a
rectangle 15 cm/6 inches by 30 cm/12 inches, cut it in
half lengthwise to give 2 strips 8 cm/3 inches by
30 cm/12 inches and then across in half and quarters
to give eight 7·5-cm/3-inch squares. Shape each
square into any of the following:

Spandauers (envelopes) Take a 7·5-cm/3-inch
square of dough and fold each corner down towards
the centre. Press gently to seal corners in centre.

Place 1 rounded teaspoon of vanilla cream in the
centre. Slip the Spandauer onto a greased baking tray
and leave to prove; then follow the baking instructions.
After baking place a spoonful of redcurrant jelly in the
centre and drizzle with white glacé icing.

Windmills Place a little almond paste in the centre of
each square, brush round the edge with beaten egg
and cut from the corners to within 1 cm/½ inch of the
centre; then fold alternate cut corners in towards the
centre, sealing them down into the almond paste.
Brush each one with egg white; place a glacé cherry
half in the centre. Place on a greased baking tray and
leave to prove.

Crèmeboller Place 1 rounded teaspoon of vanilla
cream in the centre of each square, bring the edges up
and seal together with egg white; then place upside-
down on a greased baking tray so the sealed edges
are underneath. Shape the dough into a ball. Set aside
to prove. Follow baking instructions and decorate the
tops with chocolate icing.

Tivolis Place a little apple and raisin filling diagonally
across each square then fold the uncovered corners
into the centre so they overlap slightly, sealing them
together with egg white. Lift the pastries onto the
greased baking tray and leave to prove.

Dansk Wienerbrød (Danish Pastries)

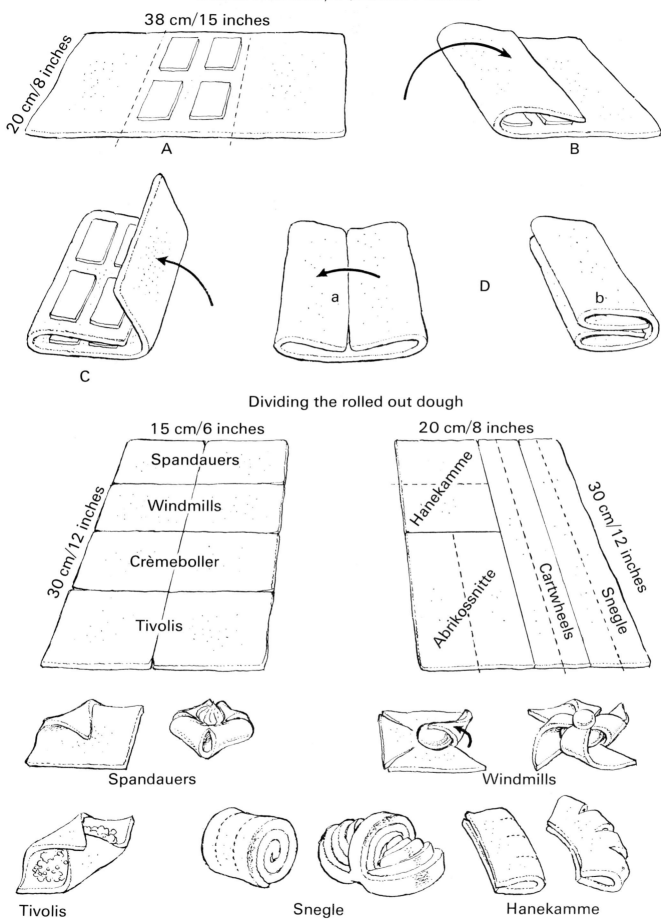

38 cm/15 inches

20 cm/8 inches

A

B

C

a

D

b

Dividing the rolled out dough

15 cm/6 inches

30 cm/12 inches

Spandauers

Windmills

Crèmeboller

Tivolis

20 cm/8 inches

Hanekamme

Abrikossnitte

Cartwheels

Snegle

30 cm/12 inches

Spandauers

Windmills

Tivolis

Snegle

Hanekamme

Roll the remaining half of the pastry dough to a rectangle 30 cm/12 inches by 20 cm/8 inches. Cut it in half lengthwise so you have 2 smaller rectangles 30 cm/12 inches by 10 cm/4 inches.

Snegle (snails) Cut the smaller rectangle in half lengthwise again to give a rectangle 30 cm/12 inches by 5 cm/2 inches. Spread this with the cinnamon sugar paste and sprinkle with a few currants. Now roll the dough up like a Swiss roll with the shortest side towards you. Cut the roll in half so you have 2 rounds about 2·5 cm/1 inch thick; slice each roll nearly all the way through in 2 places. Lay the rolls flat on a baking tray and open each out like a fan. Set aside to prove.

Cartwheels Spread the other 30-cm/12-inch by 5-cm/2-inch rectangle with almond paste, sprinkle with chopped glacé cherries and mixed peel. Roll up the dough with the short side towards you then cut the roll in half and place the rounds flat side down on the greased baking tray. Brush with beaten egg and sprinkle with chopped nuts. Set aside to prove.

Hanekamme (cocks' combs) Take the remaining half of the dough and cut in half across the length so you have smaller rectangles 15 cm/6 inches by 10 cm/4 inches. Cut this in half again so you have 2 pieces 10 cm/4 inches by 7·5 cm/3 inches. Spread chopped stem ginger or ginger marmalade lengthwise down the centres then fold over, sealing the edges together with egg white. Slash the folds about 2 cm/¾ inch deep in 4–5 different places. Place the cocks' combs on a greased baking tray, bending them slightly into a crescent so the slashes open out. Brush with egg white and sprinkle with a few chopped almonds and granulated sugar. Set aside to prove.

Abrikossnitte (apricot slips) Take the last 15-cm/6-inch by 10-cm/4-inch rectangle of dough and roll it out to make a larger and slightly thinner rectangle 20 cm/8 inches by 7·5 cm/3 inches. With the shortest side towards you spread the nearest half thickly with apricot jam then fold down the other half on top; cut in half through the fold to make two pastries 10 cm/4 inches by 4 cm/1½ inches.

Slit the top layer of dough from the centre to within 2·5 cm/1 inch of each short edge of the pastries to let the filling show through. Place the slips on a greased baking tray so that each one makes a neat rectangle; brush with egg white and sprinkle with chopped almonds or sugar crystals. Set aside to prove.

Previous pages *French Bread*

Brush the risen pastries with a little egg white and bake in the centre of a moderately hot oven (200°C., 400°F., Gas Mark 6) for 10 minutes then reduce the temperature to moderate (180°C., 350°F., Gas Mark 4) and cook for a further 15 minutes. Remove to a wire rack and drizzle white glacé icing over the pastries whilst still warm.

French Bread

Makes 2 sticks

Never quite the same as the genuine bread eaten in its country of origin – but a fair copy!

INGREDIENTS FOR STARTER DOUGH
METRIC/IMPERIAL
1 tablespoon milk
2 tablespoons water
½ teaspoon vegetable oil
½ teaspoon dried yeast
1 tablespoon warm boiled water
½ teaspoon castor sugar
1 teaspoon salt
50 g/2 oz strong white flour

INGREDIENTS FOR FRENCH BREAD
100 ml/4 fl oz milk
250 ml/8 fl oz water
1½ tablespoons vegetable oil
2 teaspoons dried yeast
4 tablespoons warm boiled water
1½ tablespoons castor sugar
525 g/1 lb 3 oz strong 81% flour
2½ teaspoons salt
starter dough (see above)
1 egg white

Prepare the starter dough: combine the milk, 2 tablespoons of water and the oil in a saucepan and bring to the boil, then cool until lukewarm. Blend the yeast in the 1 tablespoon warm boiled water with the sugar, leave aside for 5 minutes then add with the salt to cool milk mixture. Stir this liquid into the flour until it just blends thoroughly. Cover and leave to stand in a warm place for 12–18 hours.

Now prepare the bread: combine the milk, water, and oil, bring to the boil and then cool to lukewarm. Stir the yeast into the warm boiled water with ½ tablespoon of the sugar and leave aside for about 10 minutes until frothy. Place the flour in a large bowl, make a well in the centre, sprinkle the remaining sugar and the salt around the edge then pour in the milk mixture and the yeast liquid. Add the starter dough and stir until well blended to give a soft dough. *Do not knead*. Place the soft dough in a greased bowl, cover and let rise in a warm place until doubled in size, about 1 hour.

Turn the risen dough onto a well floured surface but *do not knead*. Divide the dough into 2 even pieces and roll each into an oblong about 38 cm/15 inches by 25 cm/10 inches. Roll up the rectangle tightly towards you, beginning at the wide side and sealing the edges by pinching together as you roll.

With a hand on each end, roll gently back and forth to taper the ends slightly. Place the French bread loaves on an oiled baking tray. With a sharp knife make cuts about 3 mm/⅛ inch deep diagonally along the loaf about 5 cm/2 inches apart. Let the loaves rise *uncovered* in a warm place until a little more than doubled in size. This will take about 1 hour.

Bake the bread in the centre of a hot oven (220°C., 425°F., Gas Mark 7) for 15 minutes; reduce the temperature to moderate (180°C., 350°F., Gas Mark 4) and continue for a further 15–20 minutes. Brush the tops of the loaves with the egg white mixed with 1 tablespoon cold water and return to the oven for a further 5 minutes. Remove the loaves from the oven and place on a wire rack to cool in front of an open window, in order to give a crisp crust.

Note It is really very difficult to make French bread taste just the same as it does in France, but bread flour of an 81% extraction (obtainable at health food stores) seems to give the nearest results.

Croissants au Beurre

Makes 6–12

When the Turks had encircled Budapest in their attack on that city in 1686, bakers who were working in the quiet of early morning to prepare the day's bread heard the Turks trying to tunnel their way through the city wall. The bakers raised the alarm and saved their city.

To commemorate the occasion they were asked to create a bread in the crescent shape of the emblem on the Turkish flag. Eventually the crescent rolls found their way to France where they were quickly adopted and became the favourite there that they are today. A rewarding recipe – lovely plump, buttery croissants that freeze well, too.

METRIC/IMPERIAL
25 g/1 oz lard
1 teaspoon salt
1 tablespoon sugar
150 ml/¼ pint milk
25 g/1 oz fresh yeast
3 tablespoons warm water
275 g/10 oz strong white flour
100 g/4 oz butter (at room temperature)
1 egg yolk
½ teaspoon sugar

Place the lard, salt and sugar in a bowl. Heat the milk so that it is just warm enough to melt the lard when poured over, and mix well, stirring until the lard has melted. Dissolve the yeast in 3 tablespoons warm water, add to the milk and lard mixture and stir well. Gradually work in the flour and knead everything to give a smooth but soft dough. Place the dough in a greased polythene bag and leave to rise until it has doubled in size.

Turn the risen dough out onto a lightly floured surface, knock-back and knead it lightly; then wrap in the polythene bag again and place in the refrigerator until it is cold, for about 20 minutes. The butter should be about the same consistency as the dough, so if it feels too soft and will spread easily, put it in the refrigerator to harden up, and if it is hard mash it down with a fork so that it will only just spread.

When the dough is chilled, remove from the refrigerator and roll into a long rectangle about 13 cm/5 inches by 38 cm/15 inches. Divide the butter into 3 equal parts and use one part to dab over the top two-thirds of the dough, leaving a small border. Fold the dough into 3 by bringing up the plain part of the dough over one-third of the buttered dough then folding the other piece down on top. Turn the dough so that the fold is on the right-hand side and the joins to the left. Seal the edges by pressing with your fingers. Roll out the dough to a long strip 13 cm/5 inches by 38 cm/15 inches again and cover the top two-thirds of the dough with butter and fold as before. Repeat the process again with the remaining portion of butter. Through the whole process it is important to keep the piece of dough in a rectangular shape. When all the butter has been incorporated into the dough, after the final folding into 3, place the dough in a greased polythene bag and allow to rest in the refrigerator for about 30 minutes.

(At this stage the dough can be wrapped tightly in polythene and frozen for up to 3 months. When ready to use, loosen packing and leave overnight in a refrigerator or cold place to thaw then continue as below.)

Remove the dough from the refrigerator and roll into a rectangle, repeat the folding and rolling process 3 more times, then wrap again and place in the refrigerator for a final 30 minutes. At this stage the dough can be stored overnight or even up to 3 days in the refrigerator so it is ready to make really fresh croissants at any time.

To shape the croissants: roll the dough to a rectangle 40 cm/16 inches by 28 cm/11 inches. Trim 1 cm/½ inch off this rectangle all the way round so that you are left with a rectangle 38 cm/15 inches by 25 cm/10 inches. Cut the rectangle lengthwise through the middle to give 2 strips 13 cm/5 inches by 38 cm/15 inches each. Now cut each of these into 3 equal 13-cm/5-inch squares, thus making 6 squares in all.

Start at one corner and roll each square up to the opposite corner, then twist them round into a crescent shape. To make smaller croissants, the squares may be cut diagonally in half, and then the triangles rolled up loosely towards the point, finishing with the tip underneath. Curve into a crescent shape. Place the croissants on an ungreased baking tray and brush the tops with the egg yolk, beaten with 3 teaspoons water and ½ teaspoon sugar. Cover with oiled polythene and leave at room temperature for about 30 minutes, until light and puffy. Brush again with egg wash before baking.

Bake above the centre of a hot oven (220°C., 425°F., Gas Mark 7) for 5 minutes then reduce the temperature to moderately hot (190°C., 375°F., Gas Mark 5) and continue baking for a further 15 minutes until the croissants are golden brown. Cool on a wire rack and eat as soon as possible.

Above *Basic French Brioches*
without topknots (see page 106)

Opposite *Kugelhopf (see page 106)*

French Brioche

Makes 8–10 individual brioches

The brioche is an elegant bread in a class all its own. Halfway between bread and cake, it should be eaten fresh and appreciated – never rushed. Enjoy it for breakfast with coffee or for elevenses with hot chocolate. With the topknot removed, the brioches may be stuffed with sweet or savoury sauces and eaten at dinner or luncheon.

METRIC/IMPERIAL
10 g/scant ½ oz fresh yeast or 1 teaspoon dried yeast
3 tablespoons lukewarm milk
¼ teaspoon castor sugar
225 g/8 oz strong white flour
¼ teaspoon salt
75 g/3 oz butter or margarine
15 g/½ oz castor sugar
2 large eggs, well beaten

Blend the yeast with the lukewarm milk. Stir in the ¼ teaspoon sugar and 40 g/1½ oz flour. Mix well, cover the bowl with a piece of oiled polythene and place aside in a warm place until frothy. Sift the remaining flour with the salt into a bowl, rub in the butter or margarine until the mixture resembles breadcrumbs and then add the castor sugar and beaten eggs. Stir in the yeast liquid and mix together to give a fairly stiff dough. Turn out onto a lightly floured surface and knead well. Place the dough in an oiled polythene bag and set aside in a warm place to prove. When the dough has risen, turn it out onto a lightly floured surface, knock-back and knead lightly.

Take three-quarters of the dough and roll it into 8–10 balls. Place each ball in a buttered, fluted brioche tin or deep patty tin. Roll the remaining dough into 8–10 small balls, elongating them slightly to make them pear-shaped. Press a finger into each of the larger balls in the brioche tins to make a well, then fit the stalks of the smaller balls into each one. Place the brioche tins on a baking tray and cover with oiled polythene. Set aside in a warm place until the brioches rise out of the tins then, if liked, brush them with a little beaten egg. Bake in the centre of a hot oven (220°C., 425°F., Gas Mark 7) for about 15 minutes until well risen and well browned. Cool on a wire rack.

Kugelhopf

Makes 1 large Kugelhopf which cuts into 20 slices

The Kugelhopf (or Gugelhopf) is a sweet yeast bread studded with kirsch-soaked raisins and baked in a special fluted mould. It is a native of the French province of Alsace – the Germanic name is due to the fact that the province faces Germany over the Rhine and they enjoy a good many wines and dishes in common. Baked in its special mould the Kugelhopf is very attractive to look at and delicious to eat sliced when fresh; but it stales quickly and it is then that it really comes into its own when soaked in a rum-flavoured sugar syrup. It was, in fact, used by neighbouring Lorraine as the original base for the famous Rum Baba.

METRIC/IMPERIAL
2 tablespoons kirsch (optional)
100 g/4 oz raisins, washed and dried
25 g/1 oz fresh yeast or 3 teaspoons dried yeast
275 ml/½ pint lukewarm milk
75 g/3 oz castor sugar
25 g/1 oz slivered blanched almonds
100 g/4 oz butter
2 large eggs
400 g/14 oz strong white flour
½ teaspoon salt
grated rind of 1 lemon

Spoon the kirsch over the raisins, mix well and cover and leave aside. Stir the yeast into the lukewarm milk until well blended, add 1 teaspoon of the castor sugar and leave aside for 10 minutes until frothy.

Thickly butter a large 22-cm/8¾-inch Kugelhopf tin or a 2-litre/4-pint ring mould and sprinkle in the almonds to coat the tin evenly. Cream the butter with the remaining castor sugar and gradually beat in the eggs. Add a little of the flour, then mix in the yeast liquid and work in the rest of the flour with the salt to give a very soft dough. Beat the mixture well with a wooden spoon. Work the grated lemon rind and the raisins evenly into the dough then turn it into the prepared tin so that the tin is half to two-thirds full. Cover with oiled polythene and leave aside in a warm place to rise until the dough reaches the top of the tin.

Bake in the centre of a moderately hot oven (200°C., 400°F., Gas Mark 6) for 20 minutes, then reduce the temperature to 190°C. (375°F., Gas Mark 5) and continue baking for a further 40 minutes. If the cake seems to be browning too quickly, cover the top with greaseproof paper. Leave the Kugelhopf in the tin for about 5 minutes then turn it out onto a wire rack and leave to cool.

German Courling Bread

A sweet honey bread – good to serve for tea to courting couples or otherwise!

METRIC / IMPERIAL
15 g / ½ oz fresh yeast or 1½ teaspoons dried yeast
1 teaspoon castor sugar
100 ml / 4 fl oz warm water
100 ml / 4 fl oz milk
50 g / 2 oz butter
1 teaspoon salt
100 g / 4 oz honey
450 g / 1 lb unbleached strong white flour
1 egg, beaten
TOPPING
40 g / 1½ oz fresh white breadcrumbs
1½ tablespoons demerara sugar
⅛ teaspoon salt
½ teaspoon ground cinnamon
15 g / ½ oz butter, melted

Stir the yeast and sugar into the warm water until well blended, then set aside for 10 minutes until frothy. Bring the milk to the boil, remove from the heat and stir in the butter, salt and honey. Continue stirring until the butter is melted. Stir a quarter of the flour into the milk mixture then add the yeast liquid, the egg and the remaining flour to give a very soft dough. Beat well. Cover with oiled polythene and leave to rise in a warm place for about 1½ hours and then beat well again.

While the dough is rising combine all the ingredients for the topping. Grease and lightly flour a 1·5-litre / 2¾-pint baking tin or ovenproof casserole. Turn the risen dough into the prepared tin and sprinkle with the topping. Cover again and leave to rise in a warm place until doubled in size.

Bake towards the top of a moderate oven (180°C., 350°F., Gas Mark 4) for 45 minutes, then reduce the temperature to cool (150°C., 300°F., Gas Mark 2) and continue baking for about 30 minutes (45 minutes if in a casserole). Turn onto a wire rack and leave to cool.

German Dalken

Makes 30

These crisp, miniature square doughnuts make an unusual dessert or accompaniment to coffee.

METRIC / IMPERIAL
15 g / ½ oz fresh yeast or 1½ teaspoons dried yeast
25 g / 1 oz castor sugar
150 ml / ¼ pint warm milk
300 g / 11 oz strong white flour
1 egg, beaten
25 g / 1 oz margarine, melted
deep fat for frying
icing sugar
ACCOMPANIMENTS
melted butter
damson or other jam
ground cinnamon and sugar
crumbled gingerbread
grated cheese

Stir the yeast and sugar into the lukewarm milk until well blended and leave aside for 5–10 minutes until frothy. Sift the flour into a bowl, stir in the yeast liquid, the beaten egg and the melted fat, mix to a dough and knead until it pulls away cleanly from the sides of the bowl. Place the dough in an oiled polythene bag and leave aside in a warm place to rise until doubled in size.

Turn the risen dough onto a lightly floured surface, knock-back and knead until smooth. Roll to a rectangle about 23 cm / 9 inches by 19 cm / 7½ inches and cut it into 4-cm / 1½-inch squares (by cutting 5 strips one way and then cutting across 5 times the other way). Place the dough squares on an oiled baking tray and cover with oiled polythene. Leave aside in a warm place to prove until almost doubled in size.

Meanwhile heat the fat in a deep fat fryer to 185°C. / 360°F. Fry the Dalken a few at a time until crisp and golden. Drain on absorbent paper and then dust thickly with icing sugar and serve hot with any of the accompaniments.

German Pumpernickel

A particularly good moist recipe for this popular German black bread. Wrapped in foil it keeps well and is easy to slice thinly for open sandwiches.

METRIC/IMPERIAL
150 g/5 oz (1 medium raw) potato
300 ml/½ pint water
15 g/½ oz fresh yeast or 1½ teaspoons dried yeast
1 teaspoon brown sugar
25 g/1 oz molasses or black treacle
15 g/½ oz margarine
350 g/12 oz wholewheat flour
100 g/4 oz rye flour
2 teaspoons salt
25 g/1 oz bran breakfast cereal
25 g/1 oz maize meal
½ teaspoon caraway seeds

Peel the potato, cut into quarters and cook in boiling salted water until tender; drain and mash smoothly. Leave aside to cool. Bring the water to a boil in a saucepan then pour about 4 tablespoons of the boiling water into a large bowl. Leave until it is lukewarm then stir in the yeast and brown sugar until well blended. Leave aside in a warm place for about 10 minutes until frothy. Stir the molasses or treacle and the margarine into the remaining hot water and stir until dissolved then leave aside to cool until lukewarm.

Place 100 g/4 oz of the wholewheat flour and all the rye flour in the bowl containing the yeast liquid; add the salt, bran cereal, maize meal and the cooled molasses liquid. Mix thoroughly and then beat well for at least 4 minutes (or 2 minutes with an electric mixer at high speed). Mix in the mashed potatoes and a further 50 g/2 oz of the wholewheat flour. Beat well again for a further 4 minutes to give a very thick batter. Add the caraway seeds and remaining wholewheat flour to give a fairly soft dough. Turn the dough out onto a lightly floured surface, cover the dough with the bowl and leave to rest for 15 minutes.

Knead the rested dough until smooth and elastic. This will take about 15 minutes. Place the dough in a greased bowl, cover with oiled polythene and leave to rise in a warm place until it has doubled in size. Knock-back the dough then return it to the bowl, cover, and leave to rise again for about 30 minutes. Knock-back the dough and shape into a loaf to fit into a large (1-kg/2-lb) loaf tin, cover with oiled polythene and leave to rise in a warm place until it reaches almost to the top of the tin. Bake towards the top of a moderate oven (180°C., 350°F., Gas Mark 4) for 45–50 minutes. Turn onto a wire rack and leave to cool.

Dutch Pumpernickel

This is a very solid moist bread. It should be sliced thinly to be used as a base for open sandwiches. Breakfast at a Dutch hotel or private home often consists of this type of bread with a selection of others and a variety of meats, fish and cheese for guests to make up their own platter.

METRIC/IMPERIAL
200 g/7 oz rye meal
50 g/2 oz cracked wheat
1 teaspoon salt
1 tablespoon molasses
1 tablespoon cooking oil
2 tablespoons wheat bran
450 ml/¾ pint boiling water
125 g/4 oz wholewheat flour

Place all the ingredients except the wholewheat flour in a bowl and mix thoroughly together. The mixture will be very moist. Cover the bowl with a folded damp cloth and leave overnight. The next day work into the mixture sufficient of the wholewheat flour to form a dough that is stiff enough to shape into a loaf. Turn the dough into a greased square 900-ml/1½-pint tin. Cover the tin with foil and place in a pan containing about 2·5 cm/1 inch hot water. Bake the loaf towards the bottom of a very cool oven (100°C., 200°F., Gas Mark ¼ low) for 4–5 hours until it feels solid. Refill the water in the pan as necessary.

Remove the loaf from the oven and cool completely in the tin before turning out. Wrap in damp greaseproof paper and then in foil and refrigerate for 1–2 days before slicing very thinly with a sharp knife.

German Stollen

A rich fruity folded bread. Not a traditional ingredient, but try with some lightly stewed apple folded into the centre; this keeps the bread moist and adds to the fruity flavour.

METRIC/IMPERIAL
15 g/½ oz fresh yeast or 1½ teaspoons dried yeast
¼ teaspoon castor sugar
100 ml/4 fl oz warm milk
225 g/8 oz strong white flour
¼ teaspoon salt
25 g/1 oz margarine
grated rind of 1 small lemon
50 g/2 oz chopped mixed peel
50 g/2 oz currants
50 g/2 oz sultanas
25 g/1 oz chopped blanched almonds
½ standard egg, well beaten
icing sugar

Stir the yeast and ¼ teaspoon sugar into the warm milk until well blended then add 50 g/2 oz of the flour. Cover and leave aside in a warm place until mixture is frothy. This will take about 20 minutes for fresh yeast and 30 minutes for dried yeast. Mix the remaining flour with the salt and rub in the margarine until it resembles fine breadcrumbs; then add all the prepared fruit and nuts. Add the yeast batter and the beaten egg to the flour and mix thoroughly to give a fairly soft dough.

Turn the dough out onto a lightly floured surface and knead for about 10 minutes until it is smooth and no longer sticky. Try not to add any extra flour. Place the dough in a lightly oiled polythene bag and loosely tie the ends. Leave it to rise until doubled in size. This will take 45–60 minutes in a warm place, or about 2 hours at room temperature. Turn the risen dough onto a lightly floured surface, knock-back and knead for about 3 minutes until smooth.

Roll the dough to a flat oval shape about 23 cm/9 inches by 18 cm/7 inches then mark a dent lengthwise with the rolling pin. Fold the dough over rather like folding an omelette, then place it on a greased baking sheet. Cover the Stollen with oiled polythene and leave to rise in a warm place for about 40 minutes until doubled in size.

Bake towards the top of a moderately hot oven (200°C., 400°F., Gas Mark 6) for about 30 minutes until it is well risen and browned. Place on a wire rack and leave to cool. Dust thickly with icing sugar before serving.

Greek Raisin Roll

Makes 2 loaves

Like a rather rich rolled Bath bun that can be sliced and toasted if liked, and served buttered.

METRIC/IMPERIAL
15 g/½ oz fresh yeast or 1½ teaspoons dried yeast
250 ml/8 fl oz warm milk
100 g/4 oz castor sugar
125 ml/scant ¼ pint warm water
25 g/1 oz butter, melted
2 eggs, separated
675 g/1½ lb strong white flour
½ teaspoon salt
450 g/1 lb raisins
100 g/4 oz walnuts, chopped
1 teaspoon ground cinnamon

Stir the yeast into 5 tablespoons of the warm milk with 1 teaspoon of the sugar; leave aside for about 10 minutes until frothy. In a bowl, mix the remaining milk with the water, the yeast liquid, remaining sugar, melted butter, 2 egg yolks, one of the egg whites and 450 g/1 lb of the flour. Beat this mixture together vigorously for 2–4 minutes. Cover the bowl with oiled polythene or a damp tea towel and set aside to rise for about 30 minutes. After the mixture has risen, work in the salt sieved with the remaining flour. Turn this dough onto a lightly floured surface and knead for about 5 minutes or until it is smooth and elastic. Return the dough to the bowl, cover with polythene or the damp tea towel and set aside in a warm place to rise until it has doubled in size.

Turn the risen dough out onto the floured surface, knock-back and then roll it out to a rectangle about 50 cm/20 inches long by 38 cm/15 inches wide and 1 cm/½ inch thick. Sprinkle evenly with the raisins, chopped walnuts and cinnamon and then roll the dough up like a Swiss roll. Cut it in half to make 2 rolls and place each one on a greased baking tray, with the joins underneath. Cover with oiled polythene and leave aside in a warm place to rise until doubled in size. Brush the rolls with the reserved egg white and bake towards the top of a moderate oven (180°C., 350°F., Gas Mark 4) for about 35 minutes. Cool on a wire rack and dust thickly with icing sugar before serving.

Note The bread stales rather quickly so it is best to eat on the day it is made or serve toasted when used later.

floured surface. Knead for about 5 minutes. Roll the dough into a strand approximately 45 cm/18 inches long. Coil it evenly onto a greased rectangular baking sheet. If using the hard-boiled eggs, place in the spaces of the coil. Cover the dough with oiled polythene and leave in a warm place to rise for about 1 hour or until it has doubled in size.

Brush the dough with egg wash made by lightly beating the egg yolk with the cream and then bake the bread in a moderate oven (180°C., 350°F., Gas Mark 4) for 30–40 minutes until it is well browned. When the loaf is ready the base will sound hollow when tapped. **Note** If you have used hard-boiled eggs to decorate the bread, when it is removed from the oven carefully turn it upside-down on the rack to cool, otherwise the heavy eggs can sink right through the light, hot bread dough! When the loaf is cold, brush the eggs with concentrated red food colouring so they are dyed the traditional bright red.

Lambrotsomo

Greek Easter Bread

From early history eggs have been held to have special powers and all kinds of beliefs have been built round them. To the Greeks, they are one of the most symbolic foods of the Easter table; they represent life inside the tomb. This large egg-studded loaf is really meant for a family gathering; it is worth trying half the quantity for the first time and then going gay one Easter and making the full size – perhaps with toasted red marzipan eggs instead of the boiled ones.

METRIC / IMPERIAL
200 ml / 7 fl oz lukewarm milk
175 g / 6 oz castor sugar
25 g / 1 oz fresh yeast or 3 teaspoons dried yeast
750 g / 1 lb 10 oz strong white flour
1 teaspoon salt
½ teaspoon baking powder
175 g / 6 oz butter or margarine, melted and cooled
4 eggs, lightly beaten
4 hard-boiled eggs (optional)
1 egg yolk
1 tablespoon single cream

In a large bowl combine the lukewarm milk, half the sugar and the yeast. Mix well and leave aside for about 10 minutes until frothy. Sift the flour into the yeast liquid with the salt, remaining sugar and the baking powder then add the melted butter and the lightly beaten eggs. Mix well together to form a sticky dough. Turn the dough onto a floured surface and knead well for 5 minutes until the dough becomes smooth and satiny. Form the dough into a ball and place in a greased bowl, cover with oiled polythene and leave to rise for about 2 hours or longer until it has doubled in size. Remove the dough and knock-back on a lightly

Chapati

Makes 6

The subcontinent of India is so vast with such an incredible number of different creeds and customs that accordingly many different breads are eaten. The chapati is the simplest basic form; it is an unleavened pancake-like bread eaten hot as a side bread with curries. Many of the other breads are flat (sometimes flavoured with cummin, caraway or other spices) and griddle cooked or baked, but some are deep-fried and puffed up and very light. They are all good, and eaten hot with other side dishes complement a good curry.

METRIC / IMPERIAL
225 g / 8 oz wholewheat flour
8–9 tablespoons water
butter for frying

Mix the flour in a bowl with as little of the water as possible to make a stiff dough. Knead the dough very thoroughly so that it becomes evenly blended and pliable. If necessary, a little more water may be worked in. Replace the dough in the bowl, cover with a damp cloth and leave aside for 2–3 hours.

Knead the dough again then break it into 6 equal pieces each about the size of an egg. Shape each piece into a round then flatten with your hand and roll out thinly to about 15 cm / 6 inches in diameter.

Grease and heat a griddle or a heavy frying pan and when it is very hot place a chapati carefully on it and cook for about 15 seconds, then turn the chapati over and cook it until brown spots appear on the underside. Turn it over and press it gently round the edges with a folded clean cloth until the chapati starts to rise in the centre. Remove from the griddle; butter it on one side only, and serve. To keep soft and hot wrap the chapatis in a clean tea towel.

Opposite Wholewheat Puris (see page 114), plain Nan (page 114) and Chapatis

Coconut Bread

Makes 6 round cakes

Of all the Indian breads eaten with curry this coconut bread is one of the most complementary.

METRIC/IMPERIAL
25 g/1 oz desiccated coconut
¼ teaspoon salt
50 g/2 oz strong white flour
pinch of cayenne pepper
½ teaspoon castor sugar
2 tablespoons water
50 g/2 oz fat for frying

Place the coconut, salt, flour, pepper and the sugar in a bowl. Work in about 2 tablespoons water to mix the ingredients to a fairly firm dough.

Divide into 6 small pieces and roll each out to a round about 7·5 cm/3 inches in diameter. Heat the fat in a large frying pan and fry the coconut cakes gently until they are light brown on both sides. Serve as soon as they are cooked.

Roghni Nan

Punjabi Leavened Flat Bread

Makes 4 portions

This crusty flatbread topped with toasted sesame seeds is one very good version of the many varieties of nan found in India. There the bread is cooked in the famed Tandoori oven which gives the bread its distinctive and delicious smoky taste. In this country nan is very good served with grilled food and kebabs – ideal for a barbecue when it can be warmed through on the rack to acquire something of its genuine flavour.

METRIC/IMPERIAL
5 tablespoons plain yogurt
5 tablespoons milk
1 teaspoon castor sugar
25 g/1 oz fresh yeast or 3 teaspoons dried yeast
275 g/10 oz strong white flour
¼ teaspoon salt
½ teaspoon bicarbonate of soda
1 egg, beaten
melted butter
milk
4 tablespoons sesame seeds

Place the yogurt and milk in a saucepan, lightly whisk together and then heat gently until lukewarm. Remove the pan from the heat and stir the sugar and the yeast into the lukewarm mixture. Stir until the yeast is well blended then leave aside for 5–10 minutes until frothy. Sift the flour into a bowl with the salt and bicarbonate of soda. Make a well in the centre of the flour and add the yeast liquid and the beaten egg. Work well together to form a smooth dough.

Turn the dough out onto a lightly floured surface and knead vigorously, until the dough is springy. Replace the dough in the bowl, cover with oiled polythene and place aside in a warm place until it has risen to rather less than double its size. Dust your hands with plenty of flour and divide the dough into 4 equal pieces. Roll each piece into a well shaped ball and then roll the balls out into flat oval pancakes about 5 mm/¼ inch thick and 25 cm/10 inches long.

Cover one of the upper racks of the oven with buttered kitchen foil. Brush each of the pancakes with melted butter on one side, then turn over and brush the other side with milk. Sprinkle the sesame seeds over the pancakes, then place them quickly onto the prepared top shelf of a hot oven (230°C., 450°F., Gas Mark 8). Bake for 7 minutes or until they are golden brown then remove to a wire rack. The nan are at their best eaten straight away.

Indian Semolina Pooris

Makes 6 round breads

A very light puffed up bread that makes an unusual crisp accompaniment to curries.

METRIC/IMPERIAL
50 g/2 oz strong white flour
25 g/1 oz semolina or ground rice
¼ teaspoon turmeric powder (optional)
¼ teaspoon salt
15 g/½ oz butter or margarine
1½ teaspoons plain yogurt (optional)
2–3 tablespoons water
½ teaspoon vegetable oil
7 g/¼ oz butter
1 tablespoon rice flour or ground rice
vegetable oil for frying

Sieve the flour, semolina, turmeric and salt into a bowl. Rub in the butter or margarine until the mixture resembles fine breadcrumbs. Work in the yogurt and gradually blend in sufficient water to mix to a firm dough. Turn the dough out onto a lightly floured surface and knead well for 10 minutes. Form the dough into a ball, replace it in the bowl and rub all over with the vegetable oil. Cover the bowl with a folded damp cloth and leave for at least 2 hours. (It can be kept chilled for up to 48 hours.)

Cream the butter with the rice flour. Roll out the rested dough as thinly as possible into a large circle and spread with the rice flour mixture. Roll up the circle of dough (like a carpet) into a long sausage. Roll out the sausage into a strip about 7·5 cm/3 inches by 45 cm/18 inches and using a 7·5-cm/3-inch cutter, stamp out 6 rounds.

Heat 4 cm/1½ inches vegetable oil in a heavy frying pan. When it is hot gently push 1–2 semolina pooris into the oil with a slotted spoon until submerged. As they begin to puff up, quickly turn them over and fry for 30 seconds longer. Lift out immediately onto absorbent paper and keep hot. Serve immediately.

Challah

Jewish Plaited Egg Bread

METRIC / IMPERIAL
20 g / ¾ oz fresh yeast or 2 teaspoons dried yeast
2 teaspoons castor sugar
250 ml / 8 fl oz lukewarm water
450 g / 1 lb strong white flour
1 teaspoon salt
2 eggs, beaten
1 egg yolk, beaten
poppy seeds (optional)

Stir the yeast and half the sugar into the warm water until well blended and leave aside for 5–10 minutes until frothy. Sift the flour, remaining sugar and salt together. Add the yeast liquid to 175 g / 6 oz of the sieved flour and stir until smooth and well blended. Cover the bowl with a sheet of oiled polythene and allow to rise in a warm place until doubled in size. Add the beaten eggs to the risen mixture and mix well. Work in the remaining flour to make a dough then turn the mixture out onto a lightly floured surface and knead until smooth and elastic. Place the dough in a bowl, dust the top with a little flour and cover with the oiled polythene and leave to rise again in a warm place until doubled in size. This richer mixture will take longer than usual to rise.

Knock-back and knead the risen dough for about 3 minutes then divide it into 3 equal pieces. Roll each piece on a lightly floured surface to round strips about 30 cm / 12 inches long. Work the 3 strips together at one end and plait them carefully. Place this plaited loaf on a greased baking tray, cover and allow to rise again until doubled in size, about 1 hour. Brush with the egg yolk mixed with 1 teaspoon of water, and sprinkle with poppy seeds, if liked. Bake in the centre of a moderately hot oven (200°C., 400°F., Gas Mark 6) for 10 minutes then reduce the temperature to 190°C. (375°F., Gas Mark 5) and continue baking for 35 minutes, or until the top of the loaf is delicately browned. Cool on a wire rack.

Note Instead of dividing the dough into 3 pieces it may be divided into 4 or 6 strands for plaiting (see diagrams below).

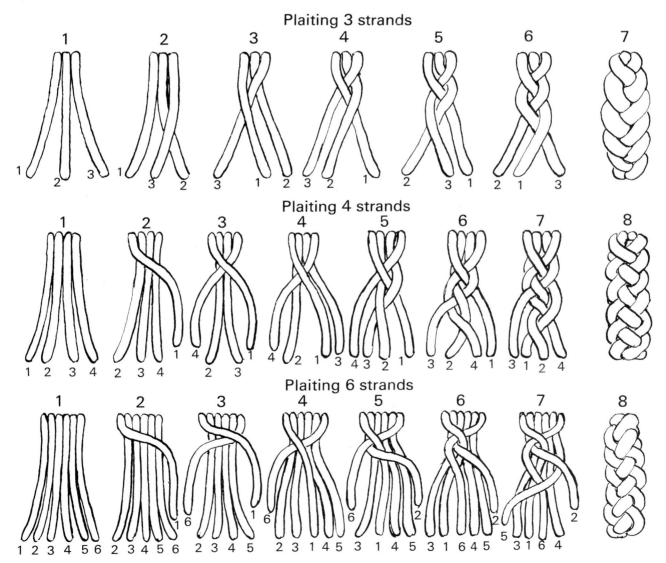

Plaiting 3 strands

Plaiting 4 strands

Plaiting 6 strands

Irish Griddle Soda Bread

Makes 4 small rounds and cuts into 8 portions

One of the joys of eating in Ireland is the great variety of breads they serve. Most families wouldn't consider the table complete without the choice of at least two or three breads. This griddle soda bread is one of the most popular; it can be served plain, toasted or fried.

METRIC/IMPERIAL
15 g/½ oz butter or margarine
225 g/8 oz plain white flour
½ teaspoon salt
½ teaspoon bicarbonate of soda
100 ml/4 fl oz milk

Rub the butter or margarine into the flour until it resembles fine breadcrumbs, then add the salt and bicarbonate and mix well together. Stir in the milk and quickly mix to a soft dough with a round-bladed knife. With well floured hands lightly knead the dough into a ball and turn out onto a floured surface. Flatten the dough to form a circle about 20 cm/8 inches in diameter and 1 cm/½ inch thick and then cut it into quarters.

Place the quarters on an ungreased griddle or in a heavy frying pan and cook them very slowly for about 15 minutes on each side until brown and when tapped on the base they sound hollow. Cool on a wire rack.

Note Instead of cooking the quarters on a griddle they may be baked in a moderately hot oven (200°C., 400°F., Gas Mark 6) for about 15 minutes.

Irish Potato Bread

Makes 12 portions

Another popular Irish bread for family meals. This pancake-like bread is good served hot or cold with butter and, if liked, a savoury spread, or it is delicious fried with bacon for breakfast.

METRIC/IMPERIAL
450 g/1 lb potatoes
50 g/2 oz butter or margarine
100 g/4 oz self-raising flour
½ teaspoon salt

Peel the potatoes and cook them in boiling salted water until tender; then drain and mash smoothly. Leave aside until cool or cold. Rub the butter into the flour until the mixture resembles breadcrumbs, add the salt and mix well. Add the potatoes and bind together with your hand.

Roll out the potato dough on a floured surface to a rectangle about 30 cm/12 inches by 23 cm/9 inches and then cut into 12 squares. Heat an ungreased griddle or heavy frying pan and cook the potato squares on both sides over a fairly high heat until they turn brown. Either eat the potato bread while it is still hot, with plenty of butter, or leave to cool in a folded tea towel before using.

Jewish Bagels

Makes 24

Bagels are best served sliced through the middle (toasted if liked) and buttered. Good with cream cheese or smoked fish – they also make an unusual breakfast roll.

METRIC/IMPERIAL
250 ml/8 fl oz milk
50 g/2 oz butter
1½ tablespoons castor sugar
½ teaspoon salt
15 g/½ oz fresh yeast or 1½ teaspoons dried yeast
1 egg, separated
400 g/14 oz strong white flour
1 teaspoon cold water
poppy seeds, sesame seeds or coarse salt crystals
(optional)

Bring the milk to the boil, remove the pan from the heat and add the butter, sugar and salt. Stir until the butter has dissolved. Pour the milk mixture into a bowl and cool until lukewarm then stir in the yeast and leave aside for 10 minutes until frothy. Beat the egg white into the yeast liquid and then gradually work in the flour. Mix together to form a smooth soft dough. Turn the dough onto a lightly floured surface and knead until smooth and no longer sticky. Form into a ball and place in an oiled polythene bag, and leave aside in a warm place for about 1 hour.

Divide the dough into 24 (25-g/1-oz) pieces and roll out to about the length of a pencil and the width of your finger, making the strips taper slightly at the ends. Shape these strips into rings, pinching the ends together. Leave the rings on the floured surface until they begin to rise. This will take about 10 minutes.

Bring a large pan of water to the boil, place the bagels a few at a time into the pan of boiling water, and cook for about 15 seconds until they puff up.

(Overcooking will cause them to break up and lose their shape, so remove quickly and carefully with a slotted spoon.)

Place the bagels on a greased baking tray. Beat the egg yolk with the teaspoon of cold water and use to brush over the bagels before baking. If liked, they may be sprinkled with poppy seeds, sesame seeds or a very few coarse salt crystals. Bake in a moderately hot oven (200°C., 400°F., Gas Mark 6) for about 20 minutes until brown and crisp. Cool on a wire rack.

La Colomba

Italian Easter Dove Bread

La Colomba is Italy's celebrated Easter dove of peace shaped loaf. Golden with egg yolks and butter, this aristocratic bread comes in all sizes from small sparrow- to great eagle-sized doves with 60-cm/2-ft wingspans. Its tail and wings may be embossed with almond paste if liked, but this tends to hide the feather pattern marked on the bird – much better to dress it with bright papers and shiny ribbons following the Italian custom and present it as an Easter gift. The origin of this loaf dates back to 1176 when two doves landed near the Milanese standards during the battle of Legnano. The Milanese read this as a sign of divine protection and went on to win the battle against the Holy Roman Empire. This victory is still remembered each year at a special Mass when two doves are released from the altar of San Simpliciano Church.

METRIC/IMPERIAL
15 g/½ oz fresh yeast or 1½ teaspoons dried yeast
2 tablespoons lukewarm water
½ teaspoon brown sugar
150 ml/¼ pint milk
100 g/4 oz butter or margarine
100 g/4 oz castor sugar
1 tablespoon grated lemon rind
2½ teaspoons vanilla essence
6 egg yolks
550 g/1¼ lb strong white flour
1 teaspoon salt
ALMOND PASTE TOPPING (OPTIONAL)
75 g/3 oz almond paste
2 egg whites
3 tablespoons castor sugar
3 tablespoons split blanched almonds

In a small bowl blend the yeast with the 2 tablespoons warm water and the brown sugar. Leave aside for 10 minutes until frothy. Bring the milk to the boil, remove from the heat and add the butter or margarine, sugar, lemon rind and vanilla essence. Stir well to dissolve the butter and then leave to cool to lukewarm. When the butter mixture has cooled, stir in the yeast liquid and the 6 egg yolks and beat well. Gradually beat in three-quarters of the flour and the salt, or sufficient to make a soft dough.

Turn the dough out onto a lightly floured surface and knead in the remaining flour. Knead for about 10 minutes or until the dough is smooth and satiny. Form the dough into a ball, put it into a greased polythene bag and put to rise in a warm place for about 1½ hours or until it has doubled in size. Knock-back the risen dough on a floured surface, knead until smooth and then divide it into 2 pieces.

Roll out half the dough into an oval about 13 cm/5 inches by 28 cm/11 inches and lay across the width of a buttered 33-cm/13-inch by 38-cm/15-inch baking tray. Roll out the remaining dough to a triangle 13 cm/5 inches wide at the base and 30 cm/12 inches long. Arrange this triangle over the oval to form a cross. Hold the triangle at the centre and twist it once, to form the body of a dove. Pinch the dough about 7·5 cm/ 3 inches below the top of the triangle to form the dove's neck and head. Elongate the tip to form the beak. With the blunt edge of a knife score the tail and wings to simulate feathers. If liked, make an almond paste topping by creaming together the almond paste with one of the egg whites and 2 tablespoons sugar then spread it thickly over the wings and tail of the dove. Leave the dough to rise in a warm place to increase its bulk a little – do not over-prove at this stage or it will lose its shape during baking.

Brush the surface of the dove with the remaining egg white, lightly beaten, and sprinkle the wings with the remaining 1 tablespoon of the sugar and the almonds, if liked. Bake the bread in a moderate oven (160°C., 325°F., Gas Mark 3) for 40–50 minutes or until it is browned. Transfer the bread carefully to wire racks and leave to cool. Serve the bread warm.

Italian Country Bread Ring

METRIC/IMPERIAL
15 g/½ oz fresh yeast or 1½ teaspoons dried yeast
6 tablespoons lukewarm water
½ teaspoon castor sugar
25 g/1 oz butter or margarine
900 g/2 lb strong white flour
1 tablespoon salt
2 egg yolks, lightly beaten
450 ml/¾ pint warm water

In a small bowl blend the yeast with 6 tablespoons lukewarm water and the sugar, then leave aside for 10 minutes until frothy. In a large bowl rub the butter or margarine into the flour until it resembles breadcrumbs. Stir in the salt. Blend the yeast liquid and the egg yolks into the dry ingredients and gradually work in sufficient of the 450 ml/¾ pint warm water to give a soft dough. Transfer the dough to an oiled polythene bag (or cover the bowl with polythene) and let the dough rise in a warm place for about 2 hours or until it has doubled in size. Knock-back the dough and knead until smooth on a floured surface.

Form the dough into a ring about 30 cm/12 inches in diameter and transfer it to a greased baking tray. Partially slice into the dough all the way round at about 5-cm/2-inch intervals. Sprinkle the bread lightly with flour then place it aside in a warm place to rise until almost doubled in size.

Bake towards the top of a moderately hot oven (200°C., 400°F., Gas Mark 6) for 10 minutes then reduce the temperature to cool (150°C., 300°F., Gas Mark 2) and continue baking for about 1½ hours longer until it is lightly browned. Turn off the heat and leave the bread to cool in the oven.

Grissini

Italian Bread Sticks

Makes 25–30

Delicious crisp Grissini – irresistible to eat with almost any meal and a great favourite with children.

METRIC/IMPERIAL
300 ml/½ pint milk
15 g/½ oz fresh yeast or 1½ teaspoons dried yeast
½ teaspoon castor sugar
450 g/1 lb strong white flour
25 g/1 oz butter or margarine, melted
1 teaspoon salt

Heat the milk to lukewarm then stir in the yeast and sugar until well blended. Measure about 100 g/4 oz of the flour into a bowl and gradually blend in the yeast liquid to make a batter. Leave aside in a warm place for about 15 minutes until frothy. Gradually blend in the melted butter or margarine followed by the remaining flour and salt to give a fairly stiff dough. Cover the bowl with oiled polythene or a plate and leave aside for about 15 minutes.

Turn the dough onto a lightly floured surface and cut into 25–30 equal pieces. Roll each of these into sticks no thicker than your little finger and 20–30 cm/8–12 inches long. Place the bread sticks on greased baking trays and leave in a warm place for about 20 minutes to rise. Brush the sticks with milk and bake towards the top of a moderate oven (180°C., 350°F., Gas Mark 4) for about 30 minutes until crisp and golden.

Panettone

A light Italian cake bread eaten throughout Italy (especially at Christmas time) with breakfast coffee. It is supposed to have originated in Milan, where in the 15th century a baker called Tony became rich and famous on the strength of a bread he made using the newly imported sultanas and candied lemon peel. The bread was known as pan de Tonio!

METRIC/IMPERIAL
50 g/2 oz castor sugar
25 g/1 oz fresh yeast or 3 teaspoons dried yeast
150 ml/¼ pint lukewarm water
3 egg yolks
½ teaspoon vanilla essence
1 teaspoon grated lemon rind
1 teaspoon salt
400 g/14 oz strong plain flour
100 g/4 oz softened butter or soft margarine
50 g/2 oz sultanas
50 g/2 oz seedless raisins
50 g/2 oz chopped mixed peel
25 g/1 oz butter, melted

Blend 1 teaspoon of the sugar and the yeast into the lukewarm water, then leave aside for about 10 minutes in a warm place until frothy. Beat the egg yolks

together in a bowl and add the yeast liquid, vanilla essence, lemon rind, salt and remaining sugar. Beat in about 225 g/8 oz of the flour then gradually beat in the softened butter or margarine about 25 g/1 oz at a time and finally beat in the remaining flour.

Turn the dough onto a lightly floured surface and knead well for about 10 minutes until it feels firm and elastic. Place the dough in a lightly oiled polythene bag and leave aside in a warm place until it has doubled in size. This will take about 1 hour.

Turn the dough out onto a floured surface, knock-back and knead in the sultanas, raisins and peel. Continue kneading until the fruit is evenly mixed in, then form the dough into a ball and place it in a greased 18-cm/7-inch deep round cake tin. Cover with the oiled polythene and leave to rise again in a warm place, until it has reached the top of the tin. This will take about 45 minutes. Brush the top of the loaf with melted butter and bake in the centre of a moderately hot oven (200°C., 400°F., Gas Mark 6) for about 20 minutes. Reduce the oven temperature to moderate (180°C., 350°F., Gas Mark 4), brush the top of the loaf again with melted butter, and continue to cook for a further 45 minutes, brushing once more with melted butter after 30 minutes. Remove the Panettone from the oven, turn out onto a wire rack and brush the top and sides with any remaining melted butter. Leave to cool. Serve, cut into thin wedges.

Italian Pizza Dough

Makes 1 pizza to serve 6 or 6 individual pizzas

This dough makes a soft, light bread base, ideal for any of the hundreds of variations of pizza toppings – seafood, meat or vegetables may all be used. Try experimenting to suit your own taste: start by putting on a garlic and tomato base, top as you please, then scatter with herbs (for authentic Italian flavour use oregano or basil) then cover with grated cheese and bake. Opposite is the recipe for one of the most popular toppings, the classic Neapolitan pizza, and below that a quick but particularly good variation.

METRIC/IMPERIAL
15 g/½ oz fresh yeast or 1½ teaspoons dried yeast
½ teaspoon castor sugar
5 tablespoons lukewarm water
50 g/2 oz butter or soft margarine
225 g/8 oz strong white flour
½ teaspoon salt
1 egg, beaten

Blend the yeast and sugar into the lukewarm water with a fork then leave aside for 10 minutes in a warm place until frothy. Rub the butter into the flour with the salt until the mixture resembles breadcrumbs. Add the yeast liquid and the beaten egg to the flour mixture and work them in together to form a stiff dough. Knead well on a lightly floured surface then place in a floured bowl and cover with an oiled polythene bag until doubled in size.

Turn the dough out onto a lightly floured surface, knock-back and either roll it into a round 30 cm/12 inches in diameter and place it on an oiled baking tray; or roll to fit a rectangular baking sheet about 23 cm/9 inches by 30 cm/12 inches; or divide the dough into 6 equal pieces and roll each to a 15-cm/6-inch round and place on greased baking trays. (The large round pizza looks effective for entertaining but do make sure it will fit into your oven!)

Pizza Napoletana

METRIC/IMPERIAL
9 tomatoes, peeled and chopped
salt and pepper
12 anchovy fillets
175 g/6 oz Mozzarella cheese (or Bel Paese), cut in thin slices
oregano or basil
2 tablespoons olive oil

Season the chopped tomatoes with salt and pepper and then spread evenly over the prepared dough. Cut the anchovies in half and arrange over the tomatoes; cover with the cheese and sprinkle with the herbs and olive oil. Bake the large pizza towards the top of a hot oven (220°C., 425°F., Gas Mark 7) for 15–20 minutes; the smaller ones will take only about 10 minutes.

Pizza alla Francesca

METRIC/IMPERIAL
225 g/8 oz mushrooms, sliced
25 g/1 oz butter or margarine
212-g/7½-oz packet processed cheese slices
226-g/8-oz can peeled tomatoes
1 clove garlic, finely chopped or crushed
298-g/10-oz can condensed tomato soup
56-g/2-oz can anchovies, cut into slivers
50 g/2 oz black olives
1 teaspoon oregano or mixed dried herbs
2 tablespoons cooking oil
Parmesan cheese (optional)

Fry the sliced mushrooms in the butter or margarine over a fairly high heat for 2–3 minutes. Arrange the cheese slices on the dough. Drain off the juice from the canned tomatoes then mash them in a bowl with the garlic and soup and spread this mixture over the cheese. Sprinkle with the fried mushrooms and arrange the anchovy slivers over in a lattice pattern. Decorate with the black olives and then sprinkle with the herbs, oil and Parmesan, if used. Bake the pizza towards the top of a hot oven (220°C., 425°F., Gas Mark 7) for about 15–20 minutes for the large pizza and about 10 minutes for the small ones.

Jordanian Kmaj

Makes 6

Individual round flat breads slightly risen with a hollow centre – good split open and stuffed with cooked meat kebabs or served with hot spicy foods. Similar bread is found all over the Middle East.

METRIC / IMPERIAL
1 teaspoon dried yeast
300 ml / ½ pint warm water
½ teaspoon castor sugar
450 g / 1 lb self-raising flour
1½ teaspoons salt

Blend the yeast into 150 ml / ¼ pint of the warm water with the sugar, and then place aside for 5–10 minutes in a warm place until frothy. Sift the flour into a large bowl with the salt, add the yeast liquid and the remaining warm water. Bind this mixture together to form a dough.

Turn out onto a lightly floured surface and knead for about 15 minutes until it is smooth and elastic and no longer sticky. Place the kneaded dough in a lightly floured bowl, and cover with oiled polythene. Leave aside in a warm place until doubled in size. Turn the risen dough out onto a floured surface, knock-back and knead until smooth and then divide into 6 equal pieces.

Roll each piece to a ball then flatten with a rolling pin and roll to rounds about 15–20 cm / 6–8 inches in diameter. Place the rounds on greased baking trays and leave aside to rise slightly.

Bake the dough rounds, a few at a time, on the upper shelf of a hot oven (220°C., 425°F., Gas Mark 7) for about 10 minutes until they puff up in the centre but are not coloured. Do not open the oven door for the first 10 minutes. Place the bread straight from the oven under a preheated hot grill to lightly brown the top only.

Latvian Saldskabmaize

A rich flavoured, sweet-sour bread as made in old Latvia.

METRIC / IMPERIAL
450 g / 1 lb strong white flour
250 ml / scant ½ pint water
2 tablespoons milk
15 g / ½ oz fresh yeast or 1½ teaspoons dried yeast
1 teaspoon castor sugar
1 teaspoon salt
2–3 teaspoons caraway seeds

Place half the flour in a warm bowl. Gradually blend in the water, which should be 90–95°C./200°F. Cover the bowl and leave aside for 10 minutes. Beat the flour mixture with a wooden spoon or wire whisk until it cools to lukewarm. Cover the bowl and leave in a warm place overnight (or for 10–12 hours). Heat the milk until it is just lukewarm. Remove from the heat and blend in the yeast and the sugar; then leave aside in a warm place for 10 minutes until frothy. Stir the yeast liquid into the flour mixture, mix in the remaining flour, salt and caraway seeds and bind together to form a dough.

Turn the dough out onto a lightly floured surface and knead well until it is no longer sticky. Roll the dough into a ball, place in an oiled polythene bag, and leave in a warm place to rise until almost doubled in size. Turn the risen dough out onto a board, knock-back and knead until smooth then shape it into a loaf about 25 cm / 10 inches long. Place on a greased baking tray and smooth the loaf over with your hand which has been dipped in cold water. Brush the loaf once more with water then bake towards the top of a moderately hot oven (200°C., 400°F., Gas Mark 6) for 45 minutes to 1 hour until it is golden brown and sounds hollow when tapped on the base.

Note To achieve a more pronounced sweet-sour effect, keep about 150 g / 5 oz of dough for a few days (see page 95) and add it with the yeast liquid.

Razih's Malaysian Roti Chanai

Makes 2 roti

Malaysia is basically a rice-eating country but, as the population has become more mixed, so their eating habits have broadened. This chapati-like bread can now claim to be Malaysian. Serve it warm as an accompaniment or base for curries – or let the children enjoy it sprinkled with sugar.

METRIC / IMPERIAL
225 g / 8 oz plain white flour
¼ teaspoon salt
8 tablespoons water
2 tablespoons melted lard or ghee
butter or margarine for frying

Mix the flour and salt in a bowl with the water to make a fairly soft but not sticky dough. Work in the melted lard or ghee. Divide the mixture in half and shape into 2 balls. Taking 1 ball at a time, place it on a working surface, flatten it and then pat and stretch it with your hand to make a round that is as large and thin as possible. (According to our Malaysian friend this should be as thin as tissue.) Work very carefully not to tear the dough, patting it to a circle about 33 cm / 13 inches in diameter or larger if you can.

Roll up the dough to make a long sausage; then, starting at one end, roll again up to the middle. Then starting at the other end roll the other side to the middle to make 2 rolls towards the centre. Upturn one roll on top of the other. Then press or roll it flat to a circle about 20 cm / 8 inches in diameter. Repeat this process with the other ball of dough then leave the rounds aside to relax for about 20 minutes. Melt a little butter or margarine in a heavy frying pan and fry rounds over a medium heat on both sides until lightly browned.

Mexican Tortillas

Makes 4 pancakes

The tortilla is a multi-purpose bread. It can be served as it is, a very thin, flat cornbread to accompany food. It can also be used as a platter or scoop for thick meat or bean mixtures; it can be fried on one side only and rolled round a chilli-and-bean stuffing to become a Taco, or stuffed, sometimes fried and coated with a sauce when it is known as an Enchillada; or finally it can be sprinkled with sweet mixtures and served as a pudding.

METRIC/IMPERIAL
225 g/8 oz polenta (maize meal)
1 teaspoon salt
225 g/8 oz plain white flour
25 g/1 oz lard or margarine
300 ml/½ pint warm water

Mix the maize meal, salt and white flour in a large bowl, add the lard or margarine and rub in until the mixture resembles breadcrumbs. Add the water and mix to a dough. Turn the dough out onto a lightly floured surface and knead for a short time until it is smooth. Shape the dough into 4 equal balls, roughly the size of a tennis ball, and let them rest for about 1 hour covered with a damp tea towel. Roll each ball out thinly on the floured surface to a circle about 25 cm/10 inches in diameter.

Heat an ungreased griddle or large frying pan and fry the maize meal pancakes over a fairly high heat, turning them over so they are lightly browned on each side.

Mongolian Kulcha

Makes 6–8 portions

This is a particularly delicious deep-fried bread. It puffs up so it is crisp on the outside and soft in the centre – excellent as an accompaniment to hot spicy food.

METRIC/IMPERIAL
200 g/7 oz strong white flour
150 ml/5 fl oz plain yogurt
1 teaspoon salt
¼ teaspoon castor sugar
1 tablespoon oil

Place all the ingredients in a mixing bowl and work together with your hands to form a dough. Knead the dough either in the bowl or on a floured surface for about 5 minutes until it is fairly smooth and elastic. Place the dough in the bowl, cover with an oiled polythene sheet and leave aside for at least 2 hours or until the food with which the Kulcha is to be served is ready to eat.

Heat a deep pan of oil to fry the Kulcha. Divide the dough into 6–8 equal pieces and roll them into balls. Roll these balls out to ovals about 15 cm/6 inches by 7·5 cm/3 inches and 5 mm/¼ inch thick. Deep-fry the Kulcha in oil for about 5 minutes or until they puff up and are golden brown, turning several times to enable them to brown evenly. Serve immediately.

Moroccan Aniseed Bread

Makes 2 small loaves

Another favourite bread with a subtle flavour and slightly chewy texture – well worth trying with butter or for making savoury sandwiches.

METRIC/IMPERIAL
15 g/½ oz fresh yeast or 1½ teaspoons dried yeast
300 ml/½ pint lukewarm water
1 teaspoon castor sugar
450 g/1 lb strong white flour
50 g/2 oz wholewheat flour
2 teaspoons salt
100 ml/4 fl oz warm milk
1 tablespoon aniseed
2 teaspoons sesame seeds

Place the yeast in a small bowl with about 3 tablespoons of the lukewarm water. Stir until well blended then mix in the sugar and place aside for 10 minutes until frothy. In a large bowl combine the white flour with the wholewheat flour and the salt. Stir in the yeast liquid and the lukewarm milk, then gradually add sufficient of the remaining lukewarm water to mix to a stiff dough.

Turn the dough out onto a lightly floured surface and knead for 15–20 minutes or until it is smooth and satiny. (If the dough becomes too dry, dampen your hand a little while kneading.) Knead in the aniseed and most of the sesame seeds.

Divide the dough in half and shape it into 2 balls; place on greased plates, cover with oiled polythene and leave to rest for about 10 minutes. With well oiled hands shape the dough into two smooth round loaves about 13 cm/5 inches in diameter, slightly domed in the centre.

Sprinkle a baking tray lightly with wholewheat flour and place the loaves on top, leaving space for them to rise, then brush the top of each loaf with water and sprinkle liberally with the reserved sesame seeds. Leave aside in a warm place to rise until almost doubled in size. Prick the risen loaves in about 4 places round the sides.

Bake in the centre of a moderately hot oven (200°C., 400°F., Gas Mark 6) for about 10 minutes then reduce the heat to a cool oven (150°C., 300°F., Gas Mark 2) and continue baking for a further 35–45 minutes until the base sounds hollow when tapped. Place the loaves on wire racks to cool.

Note Aniseed and sesame seeds are available at health food shops.

Norwegian Cornets

Makes 16 cornets or 12 rolls

This is a very light, soft bread. The cornet shapes make these dinner rolls unusual and look attractive filled with butter curls; the cornets also make a good starter or light lunch stuffed with prawns or any savoury mixture.

METRIC/IMPERIAL
400 g/14 oz strong white flour
1 teaspoon castor sugar
15 g/½ oz fresh yeast
100 g/4 oz butter or margarine
175 ml/6 fl oz tepid milk
1 egg, beaten
1 teaspoon salt

Place 200 g/7 oz of the flour, the sugar and yeast in a bowl, and rub the yeast into the flour with your fingers. Melt the butter or margarine in a saucepan, add the milk then remove from the heat and cool until lukewarm. Stir in the beaten egg then pour the mixture into the dry ingredients, beating with a fork until smooth. Cover with oiled polythene and leave aside until doubled in size. Work the remaining flour and the salt into the risen batter to make a dough.

Turn the dough out onto a lightly floured surface and knead well. Place the dough in a bowl, cover with oiled polythene and leave to rise in a warm place until it has doubled in size.

Turn the dough onto a floured surface and divide it

into 4 equal pieces. Roll each piece into a round about 20 cm/8 inches in diameter. Mark the round all over with a criss-cross pattern then cut each round into quarters. Twist each quarter, marked side out, into a greased cream horn tin. Twist pieces of kitchen foil into cornet shapes and insert them inside the dough cornets so they hold their shape. Leave the dough cornets in a warm place to rise until doubled in size.

Bake towards the top of a hot oven (220°C., 425°F., Gas Mark 7) for 10–15 minutes then remove from tins and reduce heat to moderate (180°C., 350°F., Gas Mark 4) and continue for a further 5 minutes.

Note Instead of shaping the dough into cornets, it may be divided into 12 pieces and shaped into rolls.

Norwegian Flattbröd

Makes 8 large flattbröd biscuits

Flattbröd has been made in Norway for centuries – vast quantities were prepared to be stored for the winter months. It has always been regarded as something of a ritual and in the old days a table was specially kept for making the flattbröd – often hung up under the beams of the farm kitchen and lowered for the performance! This particular flattbröd makes an excellent cheese biscuit.

METRIC/IMPERIAL
225 g / 8 oz rye flour
225 g / 8 oz wholewheat flour
½ teaspoon salt
350 ml / 12 fl oz lukewarm water

Sift the flours and salt into a bowl. Stir in sufficient lukewarm water with a wooden spoon to mix to a fairly soft dough. Turn out onto a floured surface and knead well for about 15 minutes or until a little of the dough rolled into a sausage and then bent in half will not crack. Place the dough in a greased bowl, cover with a folded damp tea towel and leave aside for at least 2 hours.

Divide the rested dough into 8 equal pieces and roll each piece into a round approximately 25 cm / 10 inches in diameter. Heat a griddle or a large frying pan and when it is very hot place one of the rounds on the heated griddle. Cook the bread until it is starting to brown in spots on the underside, then turn it over and brown the other side. Now reduce the heat and keep turning the bread until it becomes crisp. Repeat this process with all the rounds. If preferred, the rolled dough rounds may be placed on baking trays, pricked well and baked in a hot oven (220°C., 425°F., Gas Mark 7) for about 20 minutes until slightly brown and crisp.
Note Flatbreads can be made with almost any mixture of flours and with vegetables too, in the proportion of ⅕ flour to ⅘ sieved cooked root vegetables, which should be mixed, kneaded well together and made as above.

Broa

Portuguese Cornbread

A thin, light textured golden bread.

METRIC/IMPERIAL
100 g / 4 oz maize meal
1 teaspoon salt
175 ml / 6 fl oz boiling water
1 tablespoon cooking oil
15 g / ½ oz fresh yeast or 1½ teaspoons dried yeast
3 tablespoons lukewarm water
1 teaspoon castor sugar
225 g / 8 oz plain white flour

Place 75 g / 3 oz of the maize meal in a bowl with 1 teaspoon salt. Stir in the boiling water and the oil and beat the mixture until it is smooth. Then leave aside until it is lukewarm. In a small bowl blend the yeast with the lukewarm water and the sugar. Leave aside for 10 minutes until frothy. Add the yeast liquid to the maize meal mixture, and beat in the remaining maize meal and 75 g / 3 oz of the plain white flour to give a soft dough. Place the dough in an oiled polythene bag and leave aside in a warm place until doubled in size.

Turn the dough out onto a lightly floured surface, knock-back and knead in about 100–150 g / 4–5 oz of the remaining white flour, enough to make a stiff dough. Knead the dough well for about 5 minutes more until it is smooth. Brush a 20-cm / 8-inch sandwich tin lightly with oil. Pat the dough into the tin, brush it lightly with oil and leave to rise in a warm place for about 1 hour until it has doubled in size. Bake in the centre of a moderate oven (180°C., 350°F., Gas Mark 4) for 45–50 minutes until golden brown. Turn out and cool on a wire rack.

Russian Black Bread

A rich and flavoursome bread.

METRIC/IMPERIAL
300 ml / ½ pint water
½ teaspoon sugar
15 g / ½ oz fresh yeast or 1½ teaspoons dried yeast
2 tablespoons molasses or black treacle
25 g / 1 oz margarine
2 tablespoons vinegar
175 g / 6 oz wholewheat flour
75 g / 3 oz bran breakfast cereal
1½ teaspoons caraway seeds, crushed
¼ teaspoon fennel seeds, crushed
1 teaspoon salt
225 g / 8 oz rye flour
GLAZE
½ teaspoon cornflour
3 tablespoons cold water

Heat 4–5 tablespoons of the water until lukewarm then blend in the sugar and yeast. Leave aside for 10 minutes until frothy. Gently heat the molasses and margarine in a saucepan with the remaining water until dissolved, then stir in the vinegar and leave aside until lukewarm. Place the wholewheat flour, bran cereal, caraway and fennel seeds in a bowl with the salt; mix in the yeast liquid and molasses liquid and blend together to give a soft mixture; beat well. Work in the rye flour to give a fairly soft dough and then turn it out onto a lightly floured surface. Cover the dough with the bowl and leave to rest for 15 minutes before kneading well for 10–15 minutes using as little extra flour as possible.

Place the dough in an oiled polythene bag and leave aside in a warm place until it has doubled in size. Knock-back the dough, knead until smooth and then shape into a round about 15 cm/6 inches in diameter. Place the round on a greased baking tray and put to rise in a warm place until doubled in size, about 1 hour. Bake in the centre of a moderate oven (180°C., 350°F., Gas Mark 4) for 45–50 minutes.

Meanwhile combine the cornflour and the cold water and cook over a medium heat, stirring constantly, until the mixture thickens. Boil for 1 minute, stirring constantly. As soon as the bread is baked, brush the cornflour mixture over the top of the loaf. Return the bread to the oven and bake for a further 2–3 minutes or until the glaze is set. Remove the bread from the tin and cool on a wire rack.

Khachapuri

Russian Cheese Bread

Makes 1 large loaf which cuts into 12–16 portions

This rich, cheese-filled bread makes a meal in itself, delicious and filling, so only serve small portions.

METRIC/IMPERIAL
15 g/½ oz fresh yeast or 1½ teaspoons dried yeast
½ teaspoon castor sugar
3 tablespoons lukewarm water
175 ml/6 fl oz milk
100 g/4 oz butter or margarine
2 tablespoons castor sugar
1½ teaspoons salt
450 g/1 lb strong white flour
2 small eggs
FILLING
450–675 g/1–1½ lb Tilsiter or Gouda cheese, grated
50 g/2 oz butter, melted
25 g/1 oz blue cheese
2 eggs
¼ teaspoon coriander seeds, crushed
¼ teaspoon ground white pepper
GLAZE
1 egg
2 tablespoons double cream

In a small bowl blend the yeast and ½ teaspoon sugar with the lukewarm water, then place it aside for about 10 minutes until frothy. Bring the milk to a boil then pour it into a large mixing bowl. Add the butter cr margarine cut into pieces, the remaining sugar and the salt and stir until the butter is melted, then leave to cool until lukewarm. Stir in half of the flour and beat the mixture until it is smooth. Add the yeast liquid and the eggs and beat well for about 2 minutes.

Turn the mixture out onto a lightly floured surface and knead in the remaining flour. Continue to knead the dough for about 10 minutes or until it is smooth and satiny. Form the dough into a ball, put it in an oiled polythene bag and chill for at least 4 hours or overnight.

Turn the dough out onto a floured surface, knock-back and knead until smooth then roll out to a 50-cm/20-inch circle. Fold the circle lightly into quarters and put the centre point of the folded circle in the centre of a 23-cm/9-inch pie dish or tin which has been buttered and sprinkled with a little flour. Unfold the dough so that it hangs over the edge of the dish.

Make the filling by mixing the grated cheese with the melted butter, the softened blue cheese, the eggs and the crushed coriander and pepper. Spread this over the dough in the plate, mounding it slightly in the centre. Lift the sides of the dough up and arrange over the filling, pleating the dough into loose, even folds. Gather the ends of the dough in the centre and twist them into a small knot. Leave the stuffed dough aside in a warm place to rise for about 20 minutes. Brush the dough with an egg wash made by beating 1 egg with 2 tablespoons double cream or top of the milk.

Bake the bread in the centre of a moderate oven (180°C., 350°F., Gas Mark 4) for 30 minutes then reduce the temperature to 160°C. (325°F., Gas Mark 3), cover the top if necessary with paper or foil to prevent overbrowning and continue cooking for 40 minutes or until the top is golden. Leave the bread to cool in the tin for 10 minutes before turning out onto a bread board. Cut the bread into wedges and serve it warm.

Pan Mistura

This Spanish cornbread is both flavoursome and sustaining.

METRIC/IMPERIAL
300 g/11 oz strong white flour
175 g/6 oz maize meal
1½ teaspoons salt
20 g/¾ oz fresh yeast
300 ml/½ pint tepid water

Mix the flours and salt together in a bowl. Dissolve the yeast in the tepid liquid and stir into the flour. Mix to a dough and then turn it out onto a lightly floured surface and knead well. Place the dough in a greased bowl, cover with oiled polythene and set aside to rise in a warm place until doubled in size.

Turn the risen dough onto a lightly floured surface, knock-back and knead again, then shape into a flattened cob loaf. Cut a cross in the top of the loaf and place on a greased baking tray. Leave the loaf aside in a warm place to rise until doubled in size.

Bake in the centre of a hot oven (230°C., 450°F., Gas Mark 8) for about 15 minutes then reduce the heat to moderate (180°C., 350°F., Gas Mark 4) and bake for a further 20 minutes. Cool on a wire rack.

Note In Spain where Pan Mistura is made more or less daily, a piece of the dough is kept aside and soured ready for the next baking – to improve both the rise and flavour of the bread.

Place 275 g / 10 oz dough in a bowl, cover and leave aside for 3–4 days (forking it down each day) then place it in a mixing bowl with the mixed flours and warm liquid (in the proportion 275 g / 10 oz sour dough to 1 kg/2 lb flour and 500 ml/scant 1 pint water) and continue as recipe.

Ulla's
Swedish Limpa

Makes 2 large loaves

Spiced Limpa bread is eaten daily by most Swedes. It has a delicious unusual flavour which makes a good background for savoury sandwiches. It has the added advantage of keeping well.

METRIC / IMPERIAL
1 tablespoon caraway seeds
50 g / 2 oz butter
500 ml / 18 fl oz milk
40 g / 1½ oz fresh yeast
750 g / 1 lb 10 oz fine rye flour
1 tablespoon powdered fennel
1 teaspoon salt
350 g / 12 oz strong white flour
130 g / 4½ oz golden syrup
grated rind of 1 orange

Pound the caraway seeds to as near a powder as possible. This can be done with a pestle and mortar or with the handle of a rolling pin in a bowl. Heat the butter and milk together until the butter melts, then cool the mixture until just lukewarm. Crumble the yeast into the butter and milk mixture and blend it in until smooth. Place the rye flour in a bowl and stir in the yeast liquid. Sieve the fennel, caraway seeds and salt into half of the white flour then spread this spiced white flour on a working surface and turn the rye dough onto it. Knead all well together to give a smooth dough. Shape the dough into a ball, place in an oiled polythene bag and put to rise in a warm place until it is half again its size.

Warm the syrup in a saucepan until lukewarm. Turn the risen dough onto a floured surface, make holes in it with your fingers and pour in the lukewarm golden syrup. Add the remaining white flour and orange rind and knead all well together until smooth. Divide the kneaded dough in half and shape each into a rounded oblong about 25 cm / 10 inches by 9 cm / 3½ inches. Place the loaves on a greased baking tray, cover and leave to rise in a warm place until risen by half their size again. Bake in the centre of a moderately hot oven (190°C., 375°F., Gas Mark 5) for 35–45 minutes until well browned on top and the loaves sound hollow when the base is tapped. Cool on a wire rack.

Swedish Lucia Buns

Makes 15 buns and 1 plaited loaf

Lucia buns are traditionally served on December 13th. This is the Feast of St. Lucia and is really the start of the Christmas holiday in Sweden. It is the custom for a daughter of the house (if there isn't a daughter a niece or other relation may be borrowed) to dress up in a long white robe with a red belt and red stockings. On her head she has to carefully balance a crown made from pine sprigs with a ring of lit candles studded into it. Dressed like this, singing traditional songs, she makes her way from one member of the family's bedroom to the other, offering them the hot golden yellow Lucia buns with coffee.

METRIC/IMPERIAL
½ teaspoon saffron powder or 2 teaspoons turmeric powder
150 g/5 oz castor sugar
450 ml/¾ pint milk
100 g/4 oz butter or margarine
50 g/2 oz fresh yeast
900 g/2 lb strong white flour
½ teaspoon salt
½ teaspoon cardamom seeds, pounded
100 g/4 oz raisins
blanched almonds (optional)
sugar crystals (optional)

Blend the saffron or turmeric with 2 teaspoons of the castor sugar and then with 3 teaspoons of the milk. Place aside. Heat the remaining milk with the butter or margarine until this has melted. Place aside until lukewarm and then blend in the yeast until dissolved. Stir in the saffron or turmeric mixture. Place half the flour in a bowl with the salt and remaining castor sugar, stir in the yeast liquid and work in the remaining flour and the cardamom to give a moist dough. Turn onto a lightly floured surface and knead until smooth. Shape into a ball and place the dough in an oiled polythene bag. Leave in a warm place until it has doubled in size.

Turn the risen dough onto a floured surface and knead in the raisins. Now divide the dough in half and cut one half into 15 equal pieces. Each piece may be shaped into a bun using more raisins to decorate. Divide the other half into 3 strands and plait together; sprinkle with blanched almonds and sugar crystals. Place the buns and plait on greased baking trays and put to rise in a warm place until almost doubled in size. Brush the risen bread with beaten egg and then bake towards the top of a hot oven (220°C., 425°F., Gas Mark 7) for 15–25 minutes until golden brown and the bases sound hollow when tapped. Cool on a wire rack.

Tibetan Barleywheat Yeasted Loaf

A fullsome loaf with a distinctive and possibly acquired flavour!

METRIC/IMPERIAL
75 g/3 oz barley flour
15 g/½ oz fresh yeast or 1½ teaspoons dried yeast
2 teaspoons brown sugar
250 ml/8 fl oz lukewarm water
½ teaspoon salt
75 g/3 oz wholewheat flour
175 g/6 oz strong white flour
15 g/½ oz millet flakes (optional)
2 tablespoons cooking oil
cracked wheat

Spread the barley flour in a large shallow tin. Bake it in the top of a moderately hot oven (200°C., 400°F., Gas Mark 6), stirring frequently until it turns golden brown, but be careful not to overbrown or it will completely spoil the unusual toasted flavour of the finished loaf. Blend the yeast and half the sugar in the lukewarm water and place aside for 5–10 minutes until frothy. Combine the browned barley flour and salt with the other flours, remaining sugar, and millet flakes (if used). Stir in the oil and rub into the mixture so that the oil is thoroughly absorbed. Stir in the yeast liquid and mix to give a firm dough.

Knead on a lightly floured surface and then form into a ball and place in an oiled polythene bag. Leave aside in a warm place until almost doubled in size. Turn the dough out onto a lightly floured surface, knock-back and knead until smooth. Shape into a round loaf, place on a greased baking tray, brush the top with water and sprinkle with cracked wheat. Cover the loaf with oiled polythene and leave in a warm place to rise until doubled in size.

Bake towards the top of a hot oven (230°C., 450°F., Gas Mark 8) for 15 minutes then reduce the temperature to moderately hot (190°C., 375°F., Gas Mark 5) and bake for a further 20 minutes. Cool on a wire rack.

Ukrainian Kolach

Makes 2 loaves

Although this braided Kolach is enjoyed throughout the year in the Ukraine it is traditionally eaten on Christmas Eve when it forms the central table decoration at supper. A candle which has been blessed at church is placed in the middle of the Kolach and lit; it remains lit throughout the supper which consists of 12 Lenten dishes symbolising the 12 Apostles who gathered at the Last Supper.

METRIC/IMPERIAL
50 g/2 oz sugar
600 ml/1 pint water
50 g/2 oz fresh yeast or 6 teaspoons dried yeast
900 g/2 lb strong white flour
2 eggs, beaten
1 teaspoon salt
2 tablespoons cooking oil

Place the sugar in a saucepan with 150 ml/¼ pint of the water. Heat gently, stirring continuously, until the sugar has dissolved. Remove the pan from the heat and add a further 150 ml/¼ pint of the cold water. When the liquid is lukewarm, blend in the yeast. Leave it to stand for 10 minutes. Combine the yeast liquid with about a quarter of the flour and beat well together until smooth. Cover with a damp tea towel and set aside in a warm place until the mixture has sponged up and is light and bubbly. Add the well beaten eggs and the remaining water (heated to lukewarm) to the sponge mixture with the salt and oil. Work in the remaining flour to give a fairly stiff dough. Turn out and knead well on a lightly floured surface. Place the dough in an oiled polythene bag and put in a warm place to rise until doubled in size.

Remove the dough, knock-back and knead until smooth then divide the dough in half. Divide each piece of dough into 3 equal pieces and roll into long sausages. Plait the 3 strands together. Repeat with the remaining pieces of dough. Place the loaves on a greased baking tray and brush with beaten egg. Leave aside to rise in a warm place until almost doubled in size. Bake in the centre of a moderate oven (180°C., 350°F., Gas Mark 4) for about 1½ hours. Cool on a wire rack.

Overleaf *Ukrainian Kolach*

131

Ukrainian Makawnyk

Poppy Seed Roll

METRIC / IMPERIAL
25 g / 1 oz sugar
300 ml / ½ pint water
25 g / 1 oz fresh yeast or 3 teaspoons dried yeast
450 g / 1 lb strong white flour
1 egg, beaten
½ teaspoon salt
1 tablespoon cooking oil
POPPY SEED FILLING
225 g / 8 oz poppy seeds
150 g / 5 oz castor sugar
1 egg, beaten
cream or rum (optional)
icing sugar (optional)

Place the sugar in a saucepan with 4 tablespoons of the water. Heat gently, stirring continuously, until the sugar has dissolved. Remove the pan from the heat and stir in a further 4 tablespoons of cold water. When the liquid is lukewarm, blend in the yeast. Leave to stand for 10 minutes. Mix the yeast liquid with about a quarter of the flour and beat well together until smooth. Cover with a damp tea towel and set aside in a warm place until the mixture has sponged up and is light and bubbly. Add the well beaten egg and the remaining water (heated to lukewarm) to the sponge mixture with the salt and oil. Work in the remaining flour to give a fairly stiff dough. Turn out and knead well on a floured surface. Place the dough in an oiled polythene bag and put in a warm place to rise until doubled in size.

Prepare the filling by placing the poppy seeds, sugar and nearly all the beaten egg in a bowl and mixing together to make a paste; if liked a little cream or rum may be stirred in to make the filling softer. Turn the risen dough out onto a floured surface, knock-back and knead until smooth then roll out to a rectangle about 40 cm / 16 inches by 35 cm / 14 inches. Spread the poppy seed filling evenly over the dough then roll it up, starting at one of the shorter sides, like a Swiss roll. Carefully lift the poppy seed roll onto a greased baking tray and leave to rise in a warm place until it has almost doubled in size.

Brush the top of the Makawnyk with the reserved beaten egg then bake above the centre of a moderate oven (180°C., 350°F., Gas Mark 4) for about 1½ hours until golden brown. Cool on a wire rack and if liked, dust the top with icing sugar before serving.

Paska

Ukrainian Easter Bread

On Easter morning in the Ukraine, a Paska traditionally was arranged attractively in a basket with decorated eggs, a variety of cheeses, baked hams and various sausages. This was all then taken to church where it was blessed and later used for the Easter breakfast.

METRIC / IMPERIAL
200 ml / 7½ fl oz milk
100 g / 4 oz castor sugar
25 g / 1 oz fresh yeast or 3 teaspoons dried yeast
1 egg
1 egg yolk
100 g / 4 oz strong white flour
350 g / 12 oz self-raising flour
50 g / 2 oz melted butter
grated rind of 1 lemon and 1 orange
vanilla essence
50 g / 2 oz raisins or sultanas

Heat the milk until it is lukewarm. Remove from heat then add 2 teaspoons of the sugar and the yeast; stir until it is well blended then leave aside for 5–10 minutes. Beat the egg and egg yolk together until fluffy and light in colour, then add with the yeast liquid and the remaining sugar to the plain flour mixed with the self-raising flour. Mix well together then turn out onto a lightly floured surface and knead slowly and evenly for about 20 minutes. Knead in the melted butter, the lemon and orange rind, vanilla essence and raisins until evenly mixed. Shape into a ball, place in a greased polythene bag and set aside in a warm place until it has doubled in size. Remove from the bag, knock-back and knead until smooth.

Reserve a little of the dough to be used as decoration on top of the loaf and shape the rest into a ball. Place in a greased deep 18-cm / 7-inch cake tin, shape the remaining piece of dough into leaves or a cross and use to decorate the top of the loaf. Leave in a warm place until the dough has risen to the top of the tin. Bake in the centre of a moderate oven (180°C., 350°F., Gas Mark 4) for 1–1½ hours or until the base sounds hollow when tapped. Turn onto a wire rack and leave to cool.

Ukrainian Rye Bread

Makes 2 large loaves

METRIC/IMPERIAL
900 g / 2 lb rye flour
300 ml / ½ pint very hot water (not boiling)
150 ml / ¼ pint milk
25 g / 1 oz fresh yeast or 3 teaspoons dried yeast
150 ml / ¼ pint lukewarm water
2 teaspoons castor sugar
3 teaspoons salt
25 g / 1 oz butter, melted
1 tablespoon vegetable oil

Place 50 g / 2 oz rye flour in a bowl then whisk in the very hot water, stirring continuously to prevent lumps forming. Cover and leave to stand for about 1½ hours. Bring the milk to the boil, let it cool slightly then stir it into the above mixture. Beat well. Blend the yeast into the lukewarm water with 2 teaspoons sugar. Leave the yeast liquid aside for 10 minutes then add to the flour paste. Mix well and then add the salt, melted butter and oil. Work in the remaining flour to give a firm dough, rather stiffer than an ordinary bread dough.

Shape the dough into a ball, place in an oiled polythene bag and leave to rise until doubled in size. Knock-back and then put it to rise again for about 1 hour. Divide the dough into 2 pieces and shape into two large loaves. Place in greased large (1-kg / 2-lb) loaf tins and put to rise until the dough reaches the top of the tins.

Brush the tops of the loaves with beaten egg and bake towards the top of a hot oven (220°C., 425°F., Gas Mark 7) for 40–50 minutes, until the base sounds hollow when tapped. Cool on a wire rack.

Anadama Bread

Nobody quite knows how this American cornbread acquired its name. A 19th century Massachusetts story has it that there was a man whose wife, Anna, was a most unimaginative cook. She repeatedly served up cornmeal mixed with molasses: exasperated, the poor man decided to improve on this and made the mixture into a bread which he sat down to eat saying, 'Anna, damn her!'

METRIC/IMPERIAL
300 ml / ½ pint water
50 g / 2 oz maize meal
1½ teaspoons salt
75 g / 3 oz butter or margarine
100 g / 4 oz molasses or golden syrup
25 g / 1 oz fresh yeast or 3 teaspoons dried yeast
1 teaspoon castor sugar
100 ml / 4 fl oz warm water
550 g / 1¼ lb strong white flour
soft margarine to glaze
maize meal for topping

Heat the 300 ml / ½ pint water, the maize meal, salt, butter or margarine and molasses or syrup in a medium saucepan until thick and bubbly. Pour into a large bowl and leave until lukewarm. Blend the yeast and sugar into the 100 ml / 4 fl oz warm water then leave aside for 10 minutes before stirring into the cooled maize mixture. Beat in one-third of the flour until smooth, then work in sufficient of the remainder to give a stiff dough.

Turn the dough out onto a lightly floured surface and knead until smooth and elastic, using as much of any remaining flour as is necessary to keep the dough from sticking. Place the dough in a large greased bowl, cover with oiled polythene and put to rise in a warm place until it is doubled in size. Knock-back the dough and knead lightly until smooth; then shape into a ball and press into a greased 1-kg / 2-lb baking tin. Brush the top with soft margarine and sprinkle with maize meal. Put the bread to rise again in a warm place until it has doubled in size. Bake in the centre of a moderately hot oven (190°C., 375°F., Gas Mark 5) for about 50 minutes or until the loaf is golden brown and sounds hollow when the base is tapped. Remove the loaf from the tin and place on a wire rack to cool. When cold wrap in foil and store overnight before slicing.

Overleaf *American Yeasted Spoon Bread and American Graham Bread (see page 138)*

American Graham Bread

Makes 2 small loaves

METRIC/IMPERIAL
2 tablespoons brown sugar
1 teaspoon salt
25 g/1 oz butter or margarine
150 ml/¼ pint milk
15 g/½ oz fresh yeast or 1½ teaspoons dried yeast
150 ml/¼ pint lukewarm water
½ teaspoon castor sugar
450 g/1 lb graham flour (or wholewheat)
melted butter to glaze

Place the sugar, salt and butter in a saucepan with the milk, heat gently stirring continuously until the sugar has dissolved, then leave to cool until lukewarm. Blend the yeast into the lukewarm water with the castor sugar and leave aside for 10 minutes until frothy. Stir the yeast liquid into the lukewarm milk mixture, then add half of the flour and beat until smooth. Gradually work in the remaining flour to form a soft dough.

Turn the dough onto a lightly floured surface and knead until smooth and satiny. Shape into a ball, place in an oiled polythene bag and leave to rise in a warm place until it has doubled in size. Divide the dough into 2 equal pieces and shape into two small loaves. Place in well greased small (450-g/1-lb) loaf tins. Brush the dough with a little melted butter and leave to rise until doubled in size.

Bake in the centre of a moderate oven (180°C., 350°F., Gas Mark 4) for about 1 hour until evenly browned on top and the loaves sound hollow when the base is tapped. Turn out of the tins and cool on a wire rack.

American Yeasted Spoon Bread

A soft, flavourful, slightly sweet bread that can be turned out and sliced – or, as the Americans do, spooned straight from the tin and eaten with plenty of butter as an accompaniment to a meal.

METRIC/IMPERIAL
2 teaspoons dried yeast
2 tablespoons honey
250 ml/8 fl oz warm water
250 ml/8 fl oz warm milk
1 tablespoon oil
1 egg, beaten
1 teaspoon salt
200 g/7 oz maize meal
300 g/11 oz wholewheat flour

Whisk the yeast and honey into the warm water in a large mixing bowl until the honey dissolves. Then leave aside for 10 minutes until frothy. Stir the milk, oil, beaten egg and salt into the yeast liquid, making sure the yeast is dissolved, then add the maize meal and the wholewheat flour. Stir well until evenly mixed. Cover the bowl with oiled polythene and leave to rise for about 30 minutes.

Stir the risen dough to knock out the air bubbles and spoon into a greased large (1-kg/2-lb) loaf tin. Cover again and put to rise until the dough is about 2 cm/¾ inch below the top of the tin (no higher or it will overflow during cooking). Bake in the centre of a moderate oven (180°C., 350°F., Gas Mark 4) for about 50 minutes. Turn out and cool on a wire rack.

Yugoslavian Poteca

This bread ring, with its sweet moist walnut filling, is difficult to resist served hot from the oven. It is ideal to make and reheat for a coffee morning, but for normal family eating make a smaller straight Poteca by dividing the recipe in half.

METRIC/IMPERIAL
2 teaspoons dried yeast
50 g/2 oz castor sugar
3 tablespoons lukewarm water
175 ml/6 fl oz lukewarm milk
1 teaspoon salt
1 egg, beaten
50 g/2 oz soft margarine
450 g/1 lb strong white flour
WALNUT FILLING
50 g/2 oz soft butter or margarine
90 g/3½ oz demerara sugar
1 egg
3 tablespoons milk
½ teaspoon vanilla essence
rind of ½ lemon, finely grated
225 g/8 oz shelled walnuts, minced
icing sugar to decorate

Place the yeast in a mixing bowl and stir in 2 teaspoons of the sugar and the warm water; leave aside for 10 minutes then add the milk, remaining sugar, salt, beaten egg, margarine and half the flour and beat with a spoon until smooth. Add enough of the remaining flour to make a smooth soft dough, mixing it with your hand.

Turn the dough out onto a lightly floured surface and knead until it is smooth and elastic and no longer sticks to your hand. This will take about 5 minutes. Shape it into a ball, place in a greased bowl, cover with oiled polythene and put to rise in a warm place for about 2 hours or longer until doubled in size. Knockback the dough and let it rise again until it is almost doubled in size. This will take less time than before.

Prepare the walnut filling by mixing the butter or margarine with the sugar and egg; stir in the milk, vanilla essence, grated lemon rind and finally fold in the minced nuts. Mix well. Place a large sheet (or a bag split open) of polythene on your work surface and oil it. Place the dough in the centre of this and roll it out almost paper-thin to an oblong about 75 cm/30 inches by 50 cm/20 inches.

Spread the walnut filling over the thin dough, then starting at the widest edge, lift up the sheet of polythene and carefully roll up the dough and the filling, like a Swiss roll. Twist the rolled dough carefully round and seal the ends together to make a ring; place it on a greased baking tray and leave to rise in a warm place until almost doubled in size.

Bake above the centre of a moderate oven (160°C., 325°F., Gas Mark 3) for about 45 minutes until browned. Cool on a wire rack and dust the Poteca with icing sugar before serving.

Chapter 7
Breads and Teabreads without Yeast

This is a chapter of quick and easy to make breads without yeast – some savoury and some sweet. The savoury breads make a change from sandwiches for tea, supper or lunch and are delicious served with a selection of crisp salad vegetables, flavoursome spreads or soups. The sweet breads are nearly all only semi-sweet and meant to be eaten sliced and buttered as a plain teabread or with preserves.

Cracklin' Bread

The original American version of this bread used the crackling from roast pork, and, instead of flour, maize meal. If preferred, chopped pork crackling may be used instead of the streaky bacon and maize meal may be substituted for a quarter of the white flour.

METRIC/IMPERIAL
50 g/2 oz streaky bacon rashers, rinds removed
2 sticks celery, finely chopped
25 g/1 oz onion, grated
225 g/8 oz self-raising flour
¼ teaspoon salt
¼ teaspoon pepper
25 g/1 oz dripping
1 tablespoon chopped parsley
150 ml/¼ pint milk
1 small egg, beaten

Grease and line a small (450-g/1-lb) loaf tin. Finely chop the bacon then fry it for about 2 minutes in a frying pan in its own fat until crisp and golden brown. Add the chopped celery and grated onion and fry gently for a further 5 minutes until soft but not coloured; then leave aside to cool. Sift the flour into a bowl with the salt and pepper and the dripping and rub in until the mixture resembles fine breadcrumbs. Add the bacon mixture and chopped parsley to the flour, then stir in the milk and egg, beaten together.

Turn the mixture out onto a lightly floured surface and knead together lightly, then place the dough in the prepared loaf tin. Bake in the centre of a moderately hot oven (190°C., 375°F., Gas Mark 5) for about 1 hour until firm to the touch. Remove the bread from the tin and leave to cool on a wire rack before slicing and spreading with butter.

Previous pages *Cottage Cheese Liquidiser Loaf*

Celery and Peanut Teabread

Makes 1 loaf which cuts into 8 slices

METRIC/IMPERIAL
225 g/8 oz self-raising flour
½ teaspoon salt
pepper
25 g/1 oz butter or margarine
2 sticks celery, finely chopped
¼ teaspoon garlic powder (optional)
75 g/3 oz crunchy peanut butter
1 egg, beaten
150 ml/¼ pint milk

Mix the flour, salt and pepper together and rub in the butter or margarine until the mixture resembles fine breadcrumbs. Stir in the chopped celery, garlic powder and peanut butter. Add the egg and sufficient milk to mix to a stiff batter.

Spoon the batter into a greased 450-g/1-lb tin – this can be a loaf tin, empty fruit can or a cake tin. Bake above the centre of a moderately hot oven (190°C., 375°F., Gas Mark 5) for 40–50 minutes until well risen and golden brown. Leave in the tin to cool before turning out onto a wire rack; serve sliced and buttered.

Cottage Cheese Liquidiser Loaf

A light textured, mild savoury loaf – ideal for flavoursome spreads like Marmite, anchovy paste etc.

METRIC/IMPERIAL
225 g/8 oz self-raising flour
½ teaspoon salt
¼ teaspoon baking powder
25 g/1 oz sultanas, washed
50 g/2 oz celery, finely chopped
2 eggs
25 g/1 oz onion, coarsely chopped
100 g/4 oz cottage cheese
25 g/1 oz soft margarine
1–2 tablespoons milk

Grease and line a small (450-g/1-lb) loaf tin. Sift the flour, salt and baking powder into a bowl and add the sultanas and chopped celery. Place the eggs, onion, cottage cheese and margarine in the goblet of a liquidiser and switch on until all the ingredients are smoothly blended. Stir the liquidised ingredients into the flour with the milk, and mix thoroughly to give a fairly stiff, dropping consistency.

Spoon the mixture into the prepared tin and smooth the top. Bake above the centre of a moderately hot oven (190°C., 375°F., Gas Mark 5) for 40–45 minutes until well risen and golden brown. Cool the loaf in the tin for 15 minutes before turning out onto a wire rack.

French Onion Bread

Makes 1 loaf which cuts into 8 slices

This easy bread is made with a packet soup mix – in this case onion, but most mixes can be used so try others to suit your own taste.

METRIC/IMPERIAL
1 packet dried soup mix, sufficient to make
600 ml/1 pint soup
150 ml/¼ pint milk
225 g/8 oz self-raising flour
25 g/1 oz butter or margarine
1 egg, beaten
15 g/½ oz grated cheese

Grease and line a small (450-g/1-lb) loaf tin. Gradually blend the soup mix with the milk. Place the flour in a bowl and rub in the butter or margarine until the mixture resembles breadcrumbs. Stir in the soup mixture and the beaten egg and mix together to give a dropping consistency. Turn into the prepared loaf tin and sprinkle with the grated cheese.

Bake the loaf in the centre of a moderately hot oven (190°C., 375°F., Gas Mark 5) for about 1 hour until it is well risen, firm to the touch and cooked through. Turn out and cool on a wire rack.

Herb and Cheese Bread

Makes 2 small or 1 larger loaf

This flavoursome savoury bread is ideal to serve with crisp mixed salad – tomatoes, radishes, celery, watercress – or as an accompaniment to hot soup.

METRIC/IMPERIAL
225 g/8 oz self-raising flour
½ teaspoon salt
1 teaspoon dry mustard
½ teaspoon finely chopped dried or ½ tablespoon fresh mixed herbs
1 tablespoon chopped parsley (optional)
100 g/4 oz strong Cheddar cheese, finely grated
1 egg, well beaten
150 ml/¼ pint milk
25 g/1 oz butter or margarine, melted

Thoroughly grease two 500-ml/¾-pint cocoa tins or one small (450-g/1-lb) loaf tin. Sieve the flour, baking powder, salt and mustard into a bowl. Stir in the herbs, parsley and grated cheese then add the egg, milk and melted butter and mix together thoroughly. Spoon the mixture into the cocoa tins or loaf tin and bake in the centre of a moderate oven (180°C., 350°F., Gas Mark 4)

for 50–60 minutes until well risen and firm to the touch. When the herb bread is cooked, carefully remove from the tins and cool on a wire rack. Serve freshly baked.

Onion and Tomato Teabread

METRIC/IMPERIAL
225 g/8 oz self-raising flour
½ teaspoon salt
pepper
25 g/1 oz butter or margarine
1 tablespoon grated onion
2 medium tomatoes, peeled, deseeded and finely chopped
1 tablespoon chopped parsley
¼ teaspoon dried mixed herbs
1 egg
scant 150 ml/¼ pint milk

Sieve the flour, salt and pepper into a bowl and rub in the butter or margarine until the mixture resembles breadcrumbs. Add the grated onion, chopped tomato and herbs. Beat the egg and milk together, stir into the flour mixture and mix to a stiff batter. Spoon into a greased small (450-g/1-lb) loaf tin or an empty fruit can or cake tin.

Bake above the centre of a moderately hot oven (190°C., 375°F., Gas Mark 5) for 40–50 minutes until well risen and golden brown. Leave in the tin to cool before turning out onto a wire rack to serve sliced and buttered.

Peanut Butter Bread

This bread is particularly good toasted and spread with Marmite and cream cheese. Nutritious for children, too.

METRIC/IMPERIAL
100 g/4 oz self-raising flour
100 g/4 oz wholewheat flour
1 teaspoon salt
1 teaspoon baking powder
50 g/2 oz brown sugar
75 g/3 oz peanut butter
250 ml/scant ½ pint milk
25 g/1 oz salted peanuts

Grease and line a small (450-g/1-lb) loaf tin. Sieve the flours, salt and baking powder together into a bowl and add the sugar. Work in the peanut butter lightly with a fork until the mixture is crumbly and well blended. Add the milk and beat well. Turn the mixture into the prepared loaf tin and sprinkle with the salted peanuts.

Bake in the centre of a moderate oven (180°C., 350°F., Gas Mark 4) for about 1 hour until firm to the touch. Turn out onto a wire rack to cool.

Savoury Cheese, Apple and Walnut Bread

METRIC / IMPERIAL
225 g / 8 oz self-raising flour
salt and pepper
25 g / 1 oz butter or margarine
1 cooking apple, peeled, cored and finely chopped
100 g / 4 oz mature Cheddar cheese, grated
50 g / 2 oz walnuts, finely chopped
1 egg
150 ml / ¼ pint milk

Sieve the flour, salt and pepper into a bowl and rub in the butter or margarine until the mixture resembles breadcrumbs. Add the prepared apple, cheese and walnuts. Beat the egg and milk together and stir into the flour mixture to give a stiff batter. Spoon the batter into a greased small (450-g / 1-lb) loaf tin or an empty fruit can or cake tin.

Bake the savoury bread above the centre of a moderately hot oven (190°C., 375°F., Gas Mark 5) for 40–50 minutes until well risen and golden brown. Leave in the tin to cool before turning out onto a wire rack to serve sliced and buttered.

Almond Bread

Makes 1 loaf which cuts into 12 slices

A rich, sweet loaf with ground almonds.

METRIC/IMPERIAL
175 g/6 oz self-raising flour
25 g/1 oz cornflour
¼ teaspoon salt
25 g/1 oz ground almonds
150 g/5 oz soft margarine
100 g/4 oz castor sugar
3 eggs
½ teaspoon almond essence
2–3 tablespoons milk
15 g/½ oz split blanched almonds

Grease and line a large (1-kg/2-lb) loaf tin. Sieve the flour, cornflour, salt and ground almonds into a bowl. Add the soft margarine, sugar, eggs and almond essence to the dry ingredients and mix thoroughly together adding sufficient milk to give a creamy consistency. Beat for 3 minutes. Quickly spoon the mixture into the prepared tin, smooth the top and scatter with the split almonds.

Bake in the centre of a moderate oven (180°C., 350°F., Gas Mark 4) for about 1¼ hours until well risen and firm to the touch. Turn out onto a wire rack to cool.

American Muffins

Makes 9

These light muffins are a cross between a bun and a scone – delicious served with whipped cream and preserves or simply buttered warm.

METRIC/IMPERIAL
100 g/4 oz plain flour
⅛ teaspoon salt
1½ teaspoons baking powder
25 g/1 oz castor sugar
1 large egg
25 g/1 oz butter, melted
6 tablespoons milk

Grease and line 9 muffin or fairly deep patty tins. Sift the flour, salt and baking powder together into a bowl, and add the sugar. In another bowl, beat the egg with the melted butter and the milk then add to the dry ingredients and mix together quickly. Do not try to blend the ingredients smoothly together; the mixture should still be slightly lumpy.

Spoon the mixture into the prepared tins filling them two-thirds full.

Any empty tins should have a little water put in them.

Bake towards the top of a moderately hot oven (200°C., 400°F., Gas Mark 6) for about 20–25 minutes. Leave the muffins in the tins for a few moments before removing them. Eat as soon as they are taken from the tins.

Note If it is really more convenient to serve the muffins reheated, the best way to do it is to wrap them loosely in a parcel of foil and reheat in a hot oven (230°C., 450°F., Gas Mark 8) for about 5 minutes.

Apple Kuchen Bread

Makes 1 round loaf which cuts into 10 portions

This apple-topped crumble bread is ideal to serve warm with coffee or with whipped cream as a dessert.

METRIC/IMPERIAL
225 g/8 oz self-raising flour
1 teaspoon baking powder
¼ teaspoon mixed spice
150 g/5 oz brown sugar
100 g/4 oz butter or margarine
25 g/1 oz currants
1 egg
1 small can evaporated milk
225 g/8 oz cooking apples, peeled, cored and thinly sliced
2 tablespoons granulated sugar

Grease and line a fairly deep loose bottomed 23-cm/9-inch sandwich tin. Sieve the flour, baking powder and salt into a bowl, then stir in the spice and sugar. Add 75 g/3 oz of the butter or margarine and rub in until the mixture resembles breadcrumbs. Put aside 6 tablespoons of the crumb mixture for the topping. Add the currants to the remainder in the bowl. Beat the egg lightly and add to the dry ingredients with the evaporated milk and mix until evenly blended. Spoon into the prepared tin.

Arrange the apple slices in overlapping circles on top of the bread and sprinkle with the reserved crumb mixture. Dot with the remaining butter or margarine and then sprinkle evenly with granulated sugar. Bake in the centre of a moderate oven (180°C., 350°F., Gas Mark 4) for about 45 minutes until firm in the centre. Turn out and cool for 10 minutes on a wire rack then cut in wedges and serve whilst still warm.

Banana Nut Bread

A sweet banana bread good to serve sliced for tea with or without butter.

METRIC/IMPERIAL
225 g/8 oz self-raising flour
¼ teaspoon salt
50 g/2 oz margarine
50 g/2 oz castor sugar
50 g/2 oz walnuts, chopped
2 bananas
75 g/3 oz golden syrup
1 egg

Grease a large (1-kg/2-lb) loaf tin. Sift the flour and salt into a bowl, rub in the margarine until the mixture resembles breadcrumbs and then add the castor sugar and the chopped nuts. Mash the bananas with the golden syrup, and then beat in the egg. Stir the banana mixture into the dry ingredients and mix well together. Turn this mixture into the prepared loaf tin.

Bake in the centre of a moderate oven (180°C., 350°F., Gas Mark 4) for about 1 hour. Cool in the tin and when cold turn out and serve sliced with butter.

Barn Brack

Makes 1 loaf which cuts into 10 slices

A good 'all in together' sweet fruit loaf.

METRIC/IMPERIAL
225 g/8 oz mixed dried fruit
150 ml/¼ pint strained strong cold tea
225 g/8 oz self-raising flour
100 g/4 oz castor sugar
1 egg, beaten
4 tablespoons milk

Soak the dried fruit overnight in the tea in a fairly large, covered bowl. Grease and line a small (450-g/1-lb) loaf tin. Sift the flour into the fruit and tea mixture. Add the sugar and beaten egg and mix well together adding sufficient milk to give a fairly stiff consistency and turn into the prepared loaf tin.

Bake in the centre of a moderately hot oven (190°C., 375°F., Gas Mark 5) for about 40 minutes until well risen and cooked through. Turn out onto a wire rack to cool, then wrap in foil and leave overnight before slicing and spreading with butter.
Note A similar bread can be made with yeast (see page 71).

Boston Brown Bread

Makes 1 loaf which cuts into 8 slices

A rich treacle flavoured bread – good for winter teas.

METRIC/IMPERIAL
175 ml/6 fl oz milk
¼ teaspoon vinegar
1 egg, beaten
75 g/3 oz molasses or black treacle
15 g/½ oz soft margarine
50 g/2 oz castor sugar
225 g/8 oz self-raising flour
100 g/4 oz wholewheat flour
½ teaspoon salt
½ teaspoon bicarbonate of soda

Grease a small (450-g/1-lb) loaf tin or an empty coffee or fruit can. Mix the milk and the vinegar together and place aside. Beat the egg thoroughly in a large bowl

with the molasses or black treacle, the margarine and sugar. Stir well with a fork until evenly blended.

Combine the flours in a bowl then add the egg mixture with the salt, bicarbonate of soda and soured milk. Beat thoroughly and pour the batter into the prepared tin. Cover the tin tightly with a foil lid and place in a baking tin containing a little water. Bake above the centre of a moderate oven (180°C., 350°F., Gas Mark 4) for about 1 hour. Turn out onto a wire rack to cool.

Brown Date Bread

METRIC/IMPERIAL
100 g/4 oz dates, chopped
200 ml/8 fl oz boiling water
75 g/3 oz brown sugar
1 egg, lightly beaten
50 g/2 oz self-raising flour
100 g/4 oz wholewheat flour
1 teaspoon baking powder
½ teaspoon bicarbonate of soda
½ teaspoon vanilla essence
50 g/2 oz walnuts, chopped

Grease and line a small (450-g/1-lb) loaf or square tin. Place the chopped dates in a bowl and pour over the boiling water. Add the sugar to the beaten egg and then add to the sieved white and wholewheat flours with the baking powder and the bicarbonate of soda. Stir in the date mixture, the vanilla essence and the chopped nuts and mix thoroughly. Turn into the prepared tin. Bake in the centre of a moderate oven (180°C., 350°F., Gas Mark 4) for about 45 minutes. Turn out onto a wire rack to cool.

Overleaf Apple Kuchen Bread

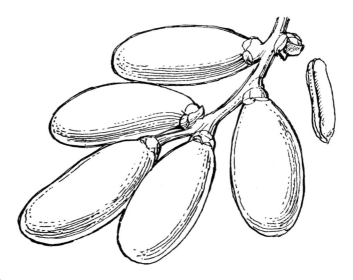

Candied Fruit Bread

METRIC/IMPERIAL
225 g/8 oz self-raising flour
1 teaspoon baking powder
½ teaspoon salt
100 g/4 oz castor sugar
2 eggs, beaten
200 ml/8 fl oz milk
3 tablespoons cooking oil
25 g/1 oz glacé cherries, finely chopped
225 g/8 oz chopped mixed peel
50 g/2 oz chopped angelica
50 g/2 oz currants

Grease and line a large (1-kg/2-lb) loaf tin. Sieve the flour with the baking powder and salt into a bowl and mix in the sugar. Combine the eggs, the milk and the oil, whisk well together then stir into the dry ingredients, beating well. Stir in the chopped glacé cherries, mixed peel, angelica and the currants and turn the mixture into the prepared tin. Bake in the centre of a moderate oven (180°C., 350°F., Gas Mark 4) for about 50 minutes.

Remove the loaf from the tin and cool on a wire rack. Wrap in foil and store overnight before slicing.

Coffee Walnut Teabread

Makes 1 loaf which cuts into 12 slices

An unusual loaf using ground coffee. It has a delicious aroma during cooking.

METRIC/IMPERIAL
225 g/8 oz self-raising flour
2 teaspoons instant coffee powder
½ teaspoon salt
150 g/5 oz soft margarine
3 eggs
150 g/5 oz demerara sugar
15 g/½ oz ground coffee
75 g/3 oz walnut pieces, coarsely minced
3–4 tablespoons milk
25 g/1 oz walnut halves

Grease and line a large (1-kg/2-lb) loaf tin. Sift the flour, instant coffee powder and salt into a large bowl, add the soft margarine, eggs, sugar, ground coffee and minced walnut pieces. Mix well together adding sufficient milk to give a creamy consistency. Beat for 3 minutes.

Quickly spoon the mixture into the prepared tin, smooth the top and stud with the walnut halves.

Bake in the centre of a moderate oven (180°C., 350°F., Gas Mark 4) for about 1¼ hours until well risen and firm to the touch. Turn out onto a wire rack.

Cream Cheese and Banana Bread

Makes 1 loaf which cuts into 10 slices

A sweet, creamy flavoured banana bread that slices well.

METRIC/IMPERIAL
100 g/4 oz castor sugar
175 g/6 oz cream cheese
25 g/1 oz butter or margarine
225 g/8 oz bananas, mashed
2 small eggs, beaten
225 g/8 oz self-raising flour
milk

Grease and line the base of a large (1-kg/2-lb) loaf tin. Cream together the sugar, cream cheese and butter or margarine until light and fluffy. Mix in the mashed bananas and the beaten eggs. Stir in the flour, then add sufficient milk to give a moist dropping consistency. Spoon the mixture into the prepared loaf tin.

Bake in the centre of a moderate oven (180°C., 350°F., Gas Mark 4) for about 1 hour until firm and well risen. Turn out onto a wire rack to cool.

Cup of Tea Loaf

Makes 1 loaf which cuts into 8 slices

METRIC/IMPERIAL
200 ml/7 fl oz cold strained tea
100 g/4 oz mixed dried fruit
1 teaspoon bicarbonate of soda
225 g/8 oz self-raising flour
75 g/3 oz granulated sugar
75 g/3 oz lard

Grease and line a large (1-kg/2-lb) loaf tin. Bring the tea and fruit to the boil in a saucepan, cover and simmer gently for 5 minutes. Remove the pan from the heat, stir in the bicarbonate of soda and leave until cold. Mix the flour and sugar together in a bowl and rub in the lard until the mixture resembles breadcrumbs. Add the soaked fruit and liquid to the dry ingredients, mix well together and spoon into the prepared tin.

Bake in the centre of a moderately hot oven (190°C., 375°F., Gas Mark 5) for about 45 minutes until well risen and cooked through. Cool the loaf in the tin for a few minutes before turning out onto a wire rack to get cold.

Dorset Apple Bread

Makes 2 rounds

A delicious apple and spice bread – at its best served straight from the griddle.

METRIC/IMPERIAL
350 g/12 oz flour
½ teaspoon salt
1 teaspoon ground cinnamon
50 g/2 oz lard
50 g/2 oz butter or margarine
50 g/2 oz castor sugar
50 g/2 oz raisins
350 g/12 oz dessert apples, peeled and coarsely grated
1 small egg
150 ml/¼ pint milk
butter for frying
demerara sugar for topping

Sift the flour into a bowl with the salt and cinnamon, then rub in the lard and butter or margarine until the mixture resembles breadcrumbs. Stir in the sugar and raisins. Add the grated apple followed by the beaten egg and sufficient milk to mix to a stiff dough.

Turn the dough out onto the floured surface and divide it in half. Shape it into 2 rounds about 20 cm/ 8 inches in diameter or to the same size as the base of your frying pan (which should be a heavy one to prevent burning). Grease a griddle or the frying pan with butter and heat it gently over a low heat then add the dough. Cook until lightly browned on one side then turn over and cook *very slowly* until brown on the other side and cooked through. To serve, split the bread open, spread with butter and sprinkle with demerara sugar. Cook the second round while the first is being eaten!

Farmhouse Fruit Loaf

Makes 1 loaf which cuts into 20 portions

METRIC/IMPERIAL
150 g/5 oz golden syrup
50 g/2 oz butter or margarine
275 g/10 oz self-raising flour
½ teaspoon salt
1 teaspoon baking powder
2 large eggs
150 ml/¼ pint milk
225 g/8 oz mixed dried fruit
grated rind of 1 lemon

Grease and line a large (1-kg/2-lb) loaf tin. Measure the syrup and butter or margarine into a saucepan and heat slowly together until melted. Sift the flour, salt and baking powder into a bowl. Beat the eggs with the milk and pour into the dry ingredients with the melted mixture. Mix thoroughly then fold in the fruit and lemon rind. Quickly spoon the mixture into the prepared tin.

Bake towards the bottom of a moderate oven (160°C., 325°F., Gas Mark 3) for about 1¼ hours. Turn out onto a wire rack and leave to cool.

Ginger Fruit Bread

Makes 1 square loaf which cuts into 16 slices

METRIC/IMPERIAL
350 g/12 oz self-raising flour
1 teaspoon baking powder
1½ teaspoons ground ginger
½ teaspoon salt
225 g/8 oz golden syrup
50 g/2 oz chopped mixed peel
75 g/3 oz raisins
100 g/4 oz soft margarine
25 g/1 oz stem ginger, chopped
25 g/1 oz glacé cherries, chopped
300 ml/½ pint milk

Grease and line a 1·75-litre/3-pint tin about 20 cm/ 8 inches square. Sift the flour, baking powder, ginger and salt into a large bowl. Add the syrup, mixed peel, raisins, soft margarine, chopped ginger, glacé cherries and about two-thirds of the milk to the dry ingredients and beat well until smoothly blended. Then mix in sufficient of the remaining milk to give a fairly soft consistency and spoon into the prepared tin.

Bake in the centre of a very cool oven (120°C., 250°F., Gas Mark ½) for 2 hours until risen and firm.
Variation Substitute 50 g/2 oz chopped walnuts for the stem ginger and glacé cherries.

Overleaf Coffee Walnut Teabread

Grace Garner's Quick Wholewheat Loaf

METRIC/IMPERIAL
1 rounded teaspoon golden syrup
250 ml/scant ½ pint hot water
1 teaspoon vinegar
225 g/8 oz wholewheat flour
225 g/8 oz plain white flour
1 teaspoon salt
1 teaspoon bicarbonate of soda
1 teaspoon cream of tartar
150 ml/¼ pint milk

Dissolve the syrup in the hot water with the vinegar and leave to cool. Grease a large (1-kg/2-lb) loaf tin. Place the wholewheat flour in a mixing bowl, sieve in the white flour with the salt, bicarbonate of soda and cream of tartar and mix well together. Add the milk to the syrup mixture and stir into the dry ingredients, as quickly as possible, to give a thick dropping consistency.

Turn this mixture into the prepared baking tin, hollowing the centre slightly so that it will rise evenly. Bake towards the top of a moderately hot oven (200°C., 400°F., Gas Mark 6) for 15 minutes, then reduce the temperature to moderate (180°C., 350°F., Gas Mark 4) for a further 20–30 minutes. Cover with greaseproof paper or foil if it is browning too quickly. Turn upside down onto a wire rack to cool, removing the tin after 5 minutes. Do not cut until the next day.

Honey Teabread

METRIC/IMPERIAL
225 g/8 oz self-raising flour
½ teaspoon salt
75 g/3 oz butter or margarine
50 g/2 oz chopped mixed peel
3 rounded tablespoons thick honey
1 small egg, beaten
150 ml/¼ pint milk

Grease and line a large (1-kg/2-lb) loaf tin. Sieve the flour and salt into a bowl and rub in the fat until the mixture resembles breadcrumbs. Stir in the peel and honey followed by the beaten egg and milk, then beat well. Place the mixture in the prepared tin.

Bake in the centre of a moderate oven (180°C., 350°F., Gas Mark 4) for about 1 hour. Leave in the tin to cool, before turning out to slice and spread with butter.

Johnnycakes

Makes 16

Johnnycake is said to be a corruption of Journeycake. In days gone by early American travellers regularly carried packets of these corn griddle breads on long trips because they kept well. They are an acquired taste.

METRIC/IMPERIAL
225 g/8 oz maize meal
1 teaspoon salt
150 ml/¼ pint boiling water
300 ml/½ pint milk

Place the maize meal and salt in a bowl, add the boiling water, then blend in the milk and mix to a stiff batter. Drop the batter 1 tablespoon at a time into a hot well greased frying pan or griddle and spread it into 7·5-cm/3-inch rounds. Fry the Johnnycakes for 1–2 minutes until the undersides are beginning to brown then turn over and cook until both sides are golden brown. Repeat to use up the remaining batter. Always serve the Johnnycakes hot with butter and, if liked, maple or golden syrup.
Note This is a traditional American Johnnycake recipe which does not include sugar – but the addition of 2 teaspoons castor sugar is an improvement.

Molasses Brown Bread

Makes 2 small loaves

METRIC / IMPERIAL
50 g / 2 oz stale breadcrumbs
3 tablespoons boiling water
100 g / 4 oz fine rye flour
2 teaspoons bicarbonate of soda
1 teaspoon salt
¼ teaspoon pepper
100 g / 4 oz maize meal
100 g / 4 oz currants
225 g / 8 oz dark molasses or black treacle
300 ml / ½ pint milk

In a large bowl fork the breadcrumbs together with the boiling water. Sieve the rye flour with the bicarbonate of soda, salt and pepper and add to the breadcrumbs with the maize meal and the currants. Whisk the molasses and milk together then quickly beat into the dry ingredients to give a batter. Pour this batter into two buttered 750-ml / 1¼-pint tins, filling each about two-thirds full.

(Empty fruit cans are ideal.)

Cover the tins or cans with a double thickness of buttered foil and tie securely. Put them in a large saucepan and add enough boiling water to reach one-third of the way up the sides of the tins. Cover the saucepan and steam the breads in gently simmering water for 3 hours. Transfer the tins to a wire rack, remove the foil and let the breads cool for 5 minutes before turning out. Leave to dry for at least 1 hour before serving.

Nut and Cherry Loaf

Makes 1 loaf which cuts into 12 slices

METRIC / IMPERIAL
100 g / 4 oz walnuts
2 eggs
75 g / 3 oz granulated sugar
7–8 tablespoons milk
350 g / 12 oz plain flour
3 teaspoons baking powder
½ teaspoon salt
50 g / 2 oz butter or margarine
25 g / 1 oz glacé cherries, halved

Grease and line a large (1-kg / 2-lb) loaf tin. Reserve a few of the nuts for decoration then finely chop the remainder or put through a mincer. Beat the eggs with the sugar and then stir in the milk. Sift the flour into a bowl with the baking powder and salt then rub in the butter or margarine until the mixture resembles bread-crumbs. Stir in the chopped nuts then add the liquid and mix thoroughly.

Turn the mixture into the prepared tin, smooth the top and decorate with the reserved whole nuts and the glacé cherries. Bake in the centre of a moderate oven (160°C., 325°F., Gas Mark 3) for about 1¼ hours until the loaf is well risen and cooked through.

If the nuts seem to be overbrowning halfway through the cooking time, cover the top with a thick piece of paper or foil.

When the loaf is cooked turn it out onto a wire rack and leave to cool. Brush sugar glaze over the cherry and nut decoration of the cake. Leave until the glaze sets. Slice the cake when it is cold and serve buttered with jam and whipped cream.

Overleaf Nut and Cherry Loaf

Orange, Date and Walnut Bread

A fairly close textured bread that is good sliced thinly and buttered, for serving after savoury sandwiches at tea.

METRIC/IMPERIAL
300 ml/½ pint milk
50 g/2 oz butter
75 g/3 oz golden syrup
350 g/12 oz plain flour
3 teaspoons baking powder
½ teaspoon salt
75 g/3 oz demerara sugar
50 g/2 oz walnuts, chopped
100 g/4 oz dates, finely chopped
grated rind of 1 orange

Grease and line a large (1-kg/2-lb) loaf tin. Warm the milk with the butter and syrup until the butter has melted. Sift the flour, baking powder and salt together into a bowl then add the sugar, chopped nuts, chopped dates and orange rind. Stir in the liquid to give a rather stiff consistency. Spoon into the prepared loaf tin and smooth the top.

Bake just above the centre of a moderate oven (180°C., 350°F., Gas Mark 4) for about 1 hour. When cooked turn the loaf out onto a wire rack and leave until cold. Serve sliced and buttered.

Prune and Honey Bread

METRIC/IMPERIAL
100 g/4 oz prunes
100 g/4 oz self-raising flour
2 teaspoons ground cinnamon
½ teaspoon baking powder
1 teaspoon bicarbonate of soda
¼ teaspoon salt
50 g/2 oz wholewheat flour
75 g/3 oz butter or soft margarine
100 g/4 oz honey
2 eggs
1 rounded teaspoon lemon rind
1 teaspoon vanilla essence
175 ml/6 fl oz soured cream or milk

Soak prunes overnight. The next day stone the prunes and chop the flesh. Grease a large (1-kg/2-lb) loaf tin thoroughly. Sift together the flour, cinnamon, baking powder, bicarbonate of soda and salt into a bowl and then stir in the wholewheat flour. In another bowl, cream the butter or margarine with the honey and eggs then add the lemon rind and vanilla essence.

Reserving 2 tablespoons of the sieved dry ingredients, beat the remainder into the egg mixture with the soured cream or milk and mix to a soft consistency. In another small bowl mix the chopped prunes with the reserved flour and then fold into the batter. Pour the mixture into the prepared loaf tin.

Bake the bread in the centre of a moderate oven (160°C., 325°F., Gas Mark 3) for about 55 minutes or until a fine skewer inserted into the centre of the bread comes out cleanly. Leave the bread to cool in the tin for about 10 minutes, then turn it out onto a wire rack and leave to cool completely.

Variation Dried apricots can be used in place of prunes.

Raisin Bran Bread

Makes 1 loaf which cuts into 12 slices

The bran makes this bread light and flavoursome.

METRIC/IMPERIAL
50 g/2 oz treacle or golden syrup
50 g/2 oz butter
100 g/4 oz wholewheat flour
2 teaspoons baking powder
1 teaspoon salt
1 teaspoon bicarbonate of soda
75 g/3 oz wheat bran
1 egg, beaten
50 g/2 oz sugar
300 ml/½ pint milk
100 g/4 oz seedless raisins

Grease and line a square 1-litre/1¾-pint tin. Place the treacle or syrup and the butter in a saucepan and heat slowly together until liquid. Sift the flour, baking powder, salt and bicarbonate of soda into a large mixing bowl. Mix in the bran then stir in the beaten egg, the sugar, milk, raisins and finally the melted syrup and butter mixture. Mix thoroughly then pour into the prepared tin.

Bake in the centre of a moderate oven (180°C., 350°F., Gas Mark 4) for about 1 hour. Leave to cool in the tin before turning out to serve.

Raisin Nut Health Bread

METRIC/IMPERIAL
1½ teaspoons baking powder
1 teaspoon salt
275 g/10 oz self-raising flour
50 g/2 oz soya flour
75 g/3 oz sugar or honey
25 g/1 oz butter or margarine
225 ml/8 fl oz milk
1 egg, lightly beaten
100 g/4 oz seedless raisins
50 g/2 oz nuts, chopped

Grease and line a large (1-kg/2-lb) loaf tin. Place the sieved baking powder, salt, flour, soya flour and sugar in a large bowl and rub in the butter or margarine until the mixture resembles fine breadcrumbs. In another bowl mix together the milk, egg and honey (if using in place of sugar). Add the liquid ingredients, the raisins and the nuts to the dry ingredients and mix well together until evenly blended. Spoon into the prepared tin and level the top.

Bake in the centre of a moderate oven (180°C., 350°F., Gas Mark 4) for about 1 hour until firm.

Rice Loaf

This loaf has an interesting crispness to its texture; it is also good with the addition of ½ teaspoon almond essence.

METRIC/IMPERIAL
100 g/4 oz margarine
100 g/4 oz castor sugar
2 eggs, beaten
finely grated rind of 1 orange
75 g/3 oz ground rice
100 g/4 oz self-raising flour
1 teaspoon baking powder
milk if necessary

Grease and line a small (450-g/1-lb) loaf tin. Cream the margarine and sugar together until light and fluffy, then gradually beat in the eggs and the orange rind. Sift the dry ingredients together and fold into the creamed mixture to give a fairly stiff dropping consistency. If it seems too dry, add a little milk to soften the batter.

Spoon the mixture into the prepared loaf tin Bake above the centre of a moderate oven (180°C., 350°F., Gas Mark 4) for about 1 hour until firm to the touch. Turn the loaf out onto a wire rack to cool and when cold, serve sliced and buttered.

Overleaf *Orange, Date and Walnut Bread*

159

Soured Cream and Walnut Bread

Makes 1 large loaf which cuts into 15–20 portions

This is a sweet, nut-topped American teabread – good cut in wedges and served with coffee.

METRIC/IMPERIAL
150 g/5 oz castor sugar
100 g/4 oz margarine or butter
3 small eggs
225 g/8 oz self-raising flour
½ teaspoon salt
¼ teaspoon baking powder
¼ teaspoon bicarbonate of soda
150 ml/¼ pint soured cream (or fresh single cream plus 1 teaspoon vinegar)
75 g/3 oz sultanas
1 teaspoon vanilla essence
TOPPING
150 g/5 oz demerara sugar
50 g/2 oz butter, softened
1 tablespoon plain white flour
½ teaspoon ground cinnamon
100 g/4 oz walnuts, chopped

Cream the castor sugar with the margarine or butter until light and fluffy, and then beat in 2 of the eggs, 1 at a time, beating well after each addition. In another bowl sieve the flour with the salt, baking powder and bicarbonate of soda. Fold half of the dry ingredients into the butter mixture, then work in the remaining egg a little at a time. Blend in the remaining flour and then fold in the soured cream, sultanas and vanilla essence. Pour this mixture into a small (450-g/1-lb) greased loaf tin.

For the topping: mix the demerara sugar with the butter, flour, cinnamon and the chopped walnuts and sprinkle over the mixture in the tin.

Bake in the centre of a moderate oven (180°C., 350°F., Gas Mark 4) for about 1 hour. Turn out onto a wire rack to cool and dust with cinnamon or more demerara sugar before serving.

Note The nut topping browns rather quickly, so to prevent it overcooking check after 40 minutes and cover the top with foil, if necessary.

Steamed Fruit and Oat Teabread

Makes 1 large or 2 smaller loaves

This bread has a good moist texture which makes it easy to slice. Useful to make when you don't want to heat the oven.

METRIC/IMPERIAL
150 ml/¼ pint milk
1 tablespoon golden syrup
½ teaspoon bicarbonate of soda
100 g/4 oz self-raising flour
50 g/2 oz wholewheat flour
¼ teaspoon salt
25 g/1 oz castor sugar
50 g/2 oz rolled oats
50 g/2 oz sultanas
25 g/1 oz walnuts, chopped

Grease an empty fruit can (or cans) which will take 750 ml–1 litre/1¼–1¾ pints. Slowly bring plenty of water to the boil in the bottom of a steamer, or sufficient water in a large saucepan to come halfway up the bread tin. Heat the milk and syrup together until the syrup has dissolved; cool, then stir in the bicarbonate of soda. Place the self-raising flour, wholewheat flour, salt, sugar and oats in a large bowl and stir in the sultanas and chopped walnuts. Pour the cooled milk mixture onto the dry ingredients and quickly mix together to give a fairly soft batter.

Spoon the mixture into the prepared tin until it is two-thirds full. Cover tightly with foil then stand the tin in the steamer or on a rack in the saucepan and steam for about 2 hours until the bread is well risen and firm. Leave the bread in the tin to cool slightly before turning out onto a wire rack to cool. When cold, slice thinly and serve buttered.

Sunshine Loaf

This loaf gets its name from its rich golden colour; it is a deliciously moist and subtly flavoured loaf that keeps well.

METRIC/IMPERIAL
175 g/6 oz self-raising flour
½ teaspoon baking powder
50 g/2 oz golden syrup
25 g/1 oz black treacle
1 rounded tablespoon orange marmalade
75 g/3 oz sultanas
100 ml/4 fl oz milk

Grease and line a small (450-g/1-lb) loaf tin. Sift the flour and baking powder into a bowl, make a well in the centre and pour in the syrup, treacle and marmalade. Add the sultanas and half of the milk. Stir to make a smooth mixture, gradually adding the remaining milk, and then spoon into the prepared tin.

Bake in the centre of a cool oven (150°C., 300°F., Gas Mark 2) for about 1¼ hours until well risen and cooked through. Turn the cooked loaf onto a wire rack to cool. Serve thinly sliced and buttered.

Sugar Plum Bread

METRIC/IMPERIAL
175 g/6 oz prunes
75 g/3 oz dried apricots
175 g/6 oz soft margarine
175 g/6 oz soft brown sugar
2 large eggs
1–2 tablespoons milk
225 g/8 oz self-raising flour
1 teaspoon baking powder
½ teaspoon salt
½ teaspoon ground cinnamon
75 g/3 oz sultanas
finely grated rind of 1 orange
granulated sugar

Place the prunes and apricots in a bowl, cover with boiling water and leave aside until cold, about 1 hour. Grease and line a large (1-kg/2-lb) loaf tin. Drain the soaked fruit and chop it fairly coarsely (after removing the stones from the prunes). Place the margarine, sugar, eggs and milk in a large bowl then add the flour sieved with the baking powder, salt and cinnamon. Beat all the ingredients together until smooth, creamy and evenly blended then stir in the chopped fruit, sultanas and orange rind.

Spoon the mixture into the prepared loaf tin, sprinkle thickly with granulated sugar and bake in the centre of a cool oven (140°C., 275°F., Gas Mark 1) for about 2½ hours. Cool the loaf in the tin slightly before turning out onto a wire rack until cold.

Overleaf Soured Cream and Walnut Bread

163

Treacle Bread

Makes 1 small round which cuts into 8 portions

METRIC/IMPERIAL
50 g/2 oz treacle or syrup
6 tablespoons milk
1 tablespoon castor sugar
½ teaspoon ground ginger
225 g/8 oz self-raising flour
¼ teaspoon salt
½ teaspoon cream of tartar
½ teaspoon bicarbonate of soda

Slowly heat the treacle until liquid and then add the milk. Mix all the dry ingredients together and make a well in the centre. Add the treacle and milk mixture to the dry ingredients and mix together to form a soft dough.

Turn the dough out onto a floured baking tray and shape into a round cake about 15 cm/6 inches in diameter with floured hands. Brush the bread with milk and bake it towards the top of a moderately hot oven (200°C., 400°F., Gas Mark 6) for 15–20 minutes, until it is risen and golden brown. Place on a wire rack and serve the treacle bread (preferably hot from the oven) split and buttered.

Vanilla Cream Bread

A delicately flavoured bread good to serve with your favourite homemade jam.

METRIC/IMPERIAL
2 large eggs, separated
150 ml/¼ pint double cream
25 g/1 oz castor sugar
½ teaspoon vanilla essence
150 ml/¼ pint milk
275 g/10 oz self-raising flour
¼ teaspoon salt

Grease a large (1-kg/2-lb) loaf tin thoroughly. Beat the egg yolks in a large bowl with the cream, sugar, vanilla essence and milk. Whisk the egg whites until very stiff. Sift the flour and salt into the egg yolk mixture, add the whisked egg whites and carefully fold all the ingredients together until evenly blended. Spoon the mixture into the prepared loaf tin.

Bake towards the top of a moderately hot oven (190°C., 375°F., Gas Mark 5) for about 40 minutes until well risen and firm to the touch.

Serve hot, cut in slices with unsalted butter.

Wheatmeal Malty

METRIC/IMPERIAL
1 teaspoon salt
275 g/10 oz wholewheat flour
175 g/6 oz plain white flour
15 g/½ oz butter or margarine
2 rounded tablespoons black treacle or golden syrup
100 g/4 oz malt extract
300 ml/½ pint water
4 teaspoons baking powder

Grease and line a large (1-kg/2-lb) loaf tin. Mix the salt into the flours in a bowl and rub in the butter or margarine until the mixture resembles breadcrumbs. Measure the treacle or syrup into a basin and stir in the malt extract and water, mixing well together. Add this liquid to the dry ingredients, mix well and then leave for 1 hour in a warm place. Sprinkle in the baking powder and stir well until evenly distributed, then turn the mixture into the prepared tin.

Bake the loaf towards the top of a moderately hot oven (200°C., 400°F., Gas Mark 6) for 15 minutes then reduce the temperature to 190°C. (375°F., Gas Mark 5) and bake for a further 25–30 minutes until the loaf is well risen and cooked through. Turn out onto a wire rack to cool.

Wheat Germ Rounds

Unusual and flavoursome scones.

METRIC/IMPERIAL
225 g/8 oz plain flour
25 g/1 oz wheat germ
3 teaspoons baking powder
½ teaspoon salt
75 g/3 oz margarine or butter
175 ml/6 fl oz milk

Mix the flour in a bowl with the wheat germ, baking powder and salt. Cut the butter into small pieces and rub them into the mixture until it resembles fine breadcrumbs. Add sufficient milk to mix to a soft dough.

Turn the dough out onto a lightly floured surface and knead lightly for a few seconds. Then roll out to about 1 cm/½ inch thick. Using a 5-cm/2-inch plain cutter, cut the dough into 12 rounds and place on greased baking trays. Bake in the centre of a moderately hot oven (200°C., 400°F., Gas Mark 6) for 10–12 minutes until golden brown. Cool on a wire rack.

Yogurt Bran Bread

METRIC/IMPERIAL
75 g/3 oz self-raising flour
75 g/3 oz wholewheat flour
25 g/1 oz bran
½ teaspoon ground cinnamon
¼ teaspoon salt
1 teaspoon bicarbonate of soda
1 egg
100 g/4 oz brown sugar
4 tablespoons cooking oil
1 rounded teaspoon grated lemon or orange rind
150 ml/5 fl oz natural yogurt

Grease and line a large (1-kg/2-lb) loaf tin. Place the flours, bran, cinnamon, salt, and bicarbonate of soda in a large bowl. In a smaller bowl beat the egg with the brown sugar, the oil, grated rind and the yogurt and pour into the dry ingredients. Quickly beat well together, and pour into the prepared loaf tin.

Bake in the centre of a moderately hot oven (190°C., 375°F., Gas Mark 5) for about 1 hour until well risen and cooked through. Turn out onto a wire rack to cool.
Note 100 g/4 oz raisins or chopped nuts may also be added to the mixture if liked.

Chapter 8
Special Diet and Health Breads

This chapter includes breads for special diets such as gluten-free and low-salt, and also breads with an increased nutritional value or increased roughage.

All breads are basically nutritious, contributing valuable quantities of protein, iron, calcium and some of the B vitamins to our diets. However, there is a small number of people who for medical reasons cannot eat 'ordinary' bread, and a growing number of people who wish to make their bread more nutritious by adding such ingredients as wheat germ and soya flour. There are also those who wish their bread to contain more roughage in the form of bran and wholewheat cereals.

The first section is for gluten-free breads, suitable for children and adults who are prescribed a gluten-free diet. These are followed by salt-free breads, for those prescribed a salt-restricted diet. The remaining recipes incorporate such ingredients as wheat germ, soya flour, bran and vegetable oils, ingredients which are readily available from health food shops and for this reason they have been called Health Breads; but, as has been pointed out above, all breads are nutritious and therefore good for one's health.

Gluten-Free Breads

These breads are suitable for those children and adults who are prescribed a gluten-free diet and who, as a result, are unable to eat ordinary bread or any breads which may contain wheat or rye flour.

It is advisable to make small loaves, as all gluten-free bread stales quickly. However, these breads freeze well when wrapped in polythene or foil, so where a freezer is available larger quantities may be prepared and any bread not for immediate use may be stored in the freezer. Breads which have begun to stale can be eaten toasted.

sugar in the warm liquid until dissolved, or dissolve the sugar in the warm liquid and sprinkle in the dried yeast. Leave to stand in a warm place until frothy, about 10 minutes.

Mix the wheat starch or gluten-free flour with the Casilan and salt and rub in the fat, until the mixture resembles breadcrumbs. Add the yeast liquid and beat well to form a smooth thick batter. Cover the bowl and allow to rise for 20 minutes. Beat the batter again thoroughly then turn the mixture into the prepared tin. Cover and prove until the mixture reaches 1 cm/½ inch below the top of the tin.

Bake in the centre of a hot oven (220°C., 425°F., Gas Mark 7) for about 30 minutes or until the centre of the loaf feels firm and springy. Turn out onto a wire rack and remove the paper. When cold, store in a polythene bag.

Plain Gluten-Free Bread

METRIC/IMPERIAL
15 g/½ oz fresh yeast or 1½ teaspoons dried yeast
1 teaspoon castor sugar
275 ml/9 fl oz warm milk and water mixed
200 g/7 oz wheat starch or gluten-free flour
25 g/1 oz Casilan* (milk protein)
1 teaspoon salt
15 g/½ oz margarine or lard

*Casilan may be obtained from most chemists.

Line a small (450-g/1-lb) loaf tin with non-stick paper or greased greaseproof paper (or this bread will be difficult to remove from the tin).

Prepare the yeast liquid: blend the fresh yeast and

Previous pages *Brown Wheat Germ Bread (see page 176) shaped into cobs*

Quick Gluten-Free Bread

Non-Yeast

METRIC/IMPERIAL
225 g/8 oz wheat starch or gluten-free flour
4 teaspoons special gluten-free baking powder*
½ teaspoon salt
50 g/2 oz margarine or lard
25–50 g/1–2 oz sugar (optional)
300 ml/½ pint milk

Line a small (450-g/1-lb) loaf tin with non-stick paper or greased greaseproof paper to prevent sticking. Sift the dry ingredients into a bowl, rub in the fat until the mixture resembles fine breadcrumbs and then stir in the sugar if used. Add the milk and mix to a soft dough. Turn into the prepared tin and spread evenly.

Bake in the centre of a hot oven (220°C., 425°F., Gas Mark 7) for about 30 minutes or until firm to the touch. Turn out onto a wire rack, remove the paper and leave to cool. Use like yeast bread.

*Mix together the following ingredients and pass through a very fine sieve 2–3 times: 75 g/3 oz cornflour, 90 g/3½ oz bicarbonate of soda, 50 g/2 oz cream of tartar, 50 g/2 oz tartaric acid (available from chemists). Store in a clearly labelled airtight container in a dry place.

Gluten~Free Cheese Bread

METRIC/IMPERIAL
15 g/½ oz fresh yeast or 1½ teaspoons dried yeast
1 teaspoon castor sugar
225 ml/7 fl oz warm milk and water mixed
200 g/7 oz wheat starch
½ teaspoon salt
50–75 g/2–3 oz Cheddar cheese, grated
1 tablespoon cooking oil

Prepare a small (450-g/1-lb) loaf tin and prepare the yeast liquid as for Plain Gluten-Free Bread (see page 170). Mix the wheat starch, salt and cheese together, add the yeast liquid and oil and beat well to form a smooth thick batter. Cover the bowl and allow to rise for 20 minutes in a warm place. Beat the batter again thoroughly then turn the mixture into the prepared tin. Cover and prove in a warm place until the mixture reaches 1 cm/½ inch below the top of the tin.

Bake in the centre of a hot oven (220°C., 425°F., Gas Mark 7) for about 30 minutes or until the centre of the loaf feels firm and springy. Turn out onto a rack, remove the paper and leave to cool.

Gluten~Free Fruit Bread

METRIC/IMPERIAL
15 g/½ oz fresh yeast or 1½ teaspoons dried yeast
½ teaspoon castor sugar
175 ml/6 fl oz warm milk and water mixed
175 g/6 oz wheat starch
25 g/1 oz castor sugar
¼ teaspoon salt
25 g/1 oz butter or margarine
50–75 g/2–3 oz mixed dried fruit

Prepare a small (450-g/1-lb) loaf tin and prepare the yeast liquid as for Plain Gluten-Free Bread (see page 170). Mix the wheat starch, sugar and salt together and rub in the fat until the mixture resembles breadcrumbs. Stir in the fruit. Add the yeast liquid to the dry ingredients and beat well to form a smooth thick batter. Cover the bowl and allow to rise for 20 minutes in a warm place. Beat again thoroughly then turn the mixture into the prepared tin. Cover and prove in a warm place until the mixture reaches 1 cm/½ inch below the top of the tin.

Bake in the centre of a moderately hot oven (190°C., 375°F., Gas Mark 5) for about 35 minutes or until the centre of the loaf feels firm and springy. Turn out onto a wire rack, remove the paper and leave to cool.

Gluten-Free Light Oatmeal Bread

METRIC/IMPERIAL
15 g/½ oz fresh yeast or 1½ teaspoons dried yeast
½ teaspoon castor sugar
150 ml/¼ pint warm milk and water mixed
175 g/6 oz wheat starch
50 g/2 oz oatmeal or rolled oats
1 teaspoon salt
1 tablespoon cooking oil
1 standard egg

Prepare a small (450-g/1-lb) loaf tin and prepare the yeast liquid as for Plain Gluten-Free Bread (see page 170). Mix the wheat starch, the oatmeal or rolled oats and salt together in a bowl. Beat the oil and egg together and add with the yeast liquid to the dry ingredients, beating well to form a smooth thick batter. Cover the bowl and allow to rise for 20 minutes in a warm place. Beat again thoroughly then turn the mixture into the prepared tin. Cover and prove in a warm place until the mixture reaches 1 cm/½ inch below the top of the tin.

Bake in the centre of a hot oven (220°C., 425°F., Gas Mark 7) for about 30 minutes or until the centre of the loaf feels firm and springy. Turn out onto a wire rack, remove the paper and leave to cool.

Salt-Free Bread

Makes 2 small loaves

This bread is suitable for those people who are prescribed a salt-restricted diet for certain medical conditions in which water tends to collect in the tissues of the body.
The method uses one rising period only because a salt-free dough becomes too sticky to handle if risen before shaping.

METRIC/IMPERIAL
15 g/½ oz fresh yeast or 1½ teaspoons dried yeast
300 ml/½ pint warm water
1 teaspoon castor sugar
450 g/1 lb strong white or brown flour or mixed flours
1 tablespoon salad oil or 25 g/1 oz salt-free butter or lard

Prepare the yeast liquid: blend the fresh yeast in the warm water until dissolved then add the sugar to the flour or dissolve the sugar in the warm water and sprinkle in the dried yeast. Set aside in a warm place until frothy, about 10 minutes. Put the flour and oil or fat in a bowl, add the yeast liquid and mix to form a dough which should be soft but firm enough to handle.

(If using a mixer and dough hook, turn the mixed dough out onto a lightly floured board and knead until smooth, about 10 minutes by hand, before shaping.)

Divide the dough into 2 equal pieces. Shape to fit two well greased small (450-g/1-lb) loaf tins. Cover with an oiled polythene bag or sheet and leave until the dough rises to the top of the tin, about 35–45 minutes in a warm place, longer in a cool place.

Bake the bread in the centre of a hot oven (230°C., 450°F., Gas Mark 8) for about 30 minutes or until the loaf has shrunk from the sides of the tin and the base of the loaf sounds hollow when tapped. Turn out onto a wire rack to cool.

Alternative shapes Dinner rolls, fancy dinner rolls and bridge rolls may be prepared from 50-g/2-oz pieces of the dough. After rising, bake towards the top of a hot oven (230°C., 450°F., Gas Mark 8) for about 15 minutes.

Variations
As salt-free bread may be insipid, herbs and other flavourings may be added to the dough to improve the flavour.

Salt-free herb bread Add 25 g/1oz chopped fresh parsley, 1 teaspoon mixed dried herbs and 2 teaspoons fresh chives.

Salt-free caraway bread Add 1–2 teaspoons caraway seeds.

Salt-free orange bread Add 1 small orange, 25 g/1 oz sugar as follows: prepare the yeast liquid by squeezing the juice from the orange and mincing the shell. Mix the juice and minced peel and make up to 300 ml/½ pint liquid with warm water. Either blend in the fresh yeast or dissolve 1 teaspoon sugar and sprinkle in dried yeast; allow to stand in a warm place until frothy. Prepare the dough as for Salt-Free Bread but add the 25 g/1 oz sugar to the flour before mixing.

Health Breads

High Protein Bread (1)

Makes 1 large and 1 small loaf or 3 small loaves

This bread is enriched with soya flour, wheat germ and rolled oats.

METRIC/IMPERIAL
15 g/½ oz fresh yeast or 1½ teaspoons dried yeast
50 ml/2 fl oz warm water
1 teaspoon soft brown sugar
75 g/3 oz rolled oats
2 teaspoons salt
450 ml/¾ pint skimmed milk
4 tablespoons cooking oil
25 g/1 oz soft brown sugar
40 g/1½ oz wheat germ
75 g/3 oz soya flour
275 g/10 oz wholewheat flour
400 g/14 oz strong white flour

Prepare the yeast liquid: blend the fresh yeast in the warm water until dissolved or dissolve the sugar in the warm water, sprinkle in the dried yeast and leave in a warm place for 10 minutes until dissolved and frothy. Put the rolled oats and salt in a large bowl. Heat the milk to boiling point and pour into the bowl. Add the oil and sugar and leave the oats to cool until lukewarm. Add the yeast liquid to the cooled mixture with the remaining dry ingredients. Mix to form a soft dough.

Turn the dough out onto a lightly floured surface and knead until smooth and elastic. Place inside an oiled polythene bag and leave to rise until doubled in size. Knock-back and knead until the dough is firm, about 2 minutes. Divide the dough into 3 equal pieces to make small loaves or cut off two-thirds for a large loaf and one-third for a small loaf. Shape to fit three small (450-g/1-lb) loaf tins or one large (1-kg/2-lb) tin and one small tin. Cover and prove for about 1 hour in a warm place.

Bake the loaves in the centre of a moderate oven (180°C., 350°F., Gas Mark 4), allowing 45–50 minutes for a large loaf and 30–35 minutes for small loaves.

High Protein Bread (2)

Makes 1 large or 2 small loaves

This bread is enriched with soya flour, wheat germ and dried skimmed milk.

METRIC/IMPERIAL
15 g/½ oz fresh yeast or 1½ teaspoons dried yeast
1 tablespoon honey
350 ml/12 fl oz warm water
175 g/6 oz wholewheat flour
350 g/12 oz unbleached white flour
25 g/1 oz soya flour
2 tablespoons wheat germ
40 g/1½ oz non-fat dry milk
2 teaspoons salt
1 tablespoon vegetable oil

Prepare the yeast liquid: blend the fresh yeast and honey in the warm water until dissolved, or dissolve the honey in the warm water and sprinkle in the dried yeast; and leave in a warm place for about 10 minutes or until dissolved and frothy. Mix the flours, wheat germ, non-fat dry milk and salt together in a large bowl. Add the yeast liquid and oil and mix to a soft dough, adding more flour if too sticky to handle.

Turn the dough out onto a lightly floured surface and knead until smooth and elastic. Put to rise and knock-back as for High Protein Bread (1). Shape to fit a well greased large (1-kg/2-lb) loaf tin, or divide into 2 pieces and shape to fit two well greased small (450-g/1-lb) loaf tins. Cover and prove for about 1 hour in a warm place, longer in a cool place.

Bake the loaves in the centre of a moderate oven (180°C., 350°F., Gas Mark 4), allowing 45–50 minutes for a large loaf and 30–35 minutes for small loaves. Turn onto a wire rack to cool.

Overleaf Salt-Free Herb Bread

Soya Flour Bread

Makes 1 large or 2 small loaves

This is a white bread with some of the wheat flour replaced by soya flour to produce a bread with a rich creamy colour, a soft texture and a higher protein value.
Soya flour does not contain gluten and breads made with it have a closer texture than breads made only from wheat flour; however, the texture is improved if additional rising and kneading periods are incorporated into the method (see below).

METRIC/IMPERIAL
15 g/½ oz fresh yeast or 1½ teaspoons dried yeast
250 ml/8 fl oz warm skimmed milk
2 tablespoons castor sugar
350 g/12 oz strong white flour
100 g/4 oz soya flour
2 teaspoons salt
25 g/1 oz butter or margarine
1 standard egg, beaten

Prepare the yeast liquid: dissolve the fresh yeast in warm milk in a large bowl or sprinkle the dried yeast and 1 teaspoon sugar into the warm milk and leave to stand in a warm place until dissolved and frothy, about 10 minutes. Mix the white flour, soya flour and salt together in a bowl and rub in the butter or margarine until the mixture resembles breadcrumbs, then add the sugar. Add the flour mixture to the yeast liquid with the beaten egg and mix to form a soft dough, adding extra flour if it is too sticky to handle.

Turn out onto a lightly floured surface, and knead for about 10 minutes. Place the dough inside a large oiled polythene bag and leave to rise in a warm place for 30 minutes. Remove from the polythene bag and knead again for 1 minute. Repeat the rising and kneading process twice more. Shape to fit a well greased large (1-kg/2-lb) loaf tin, or divide the dough into 2 pieces and shape to fit two well greased small (450-g/1-lb) loaf tins. Cover and prove for about 1 hour in a warm place, when the dough should have risen above the top of the tins.

Bake in the centre of a moderately hot oven (190°C., 375°F., Gas Mark 5), allowing 40–45 minutes for a large loaf and 30–35 minutes for small loaves.
Variation Replace 175 g/6 oz white flour with wholewheat flour.

Brown Wheat Germ Bread

Makes 1 large or 2 small loaves

This is wheatmeal bread enriched with wheat germ.

METRIC/IMPERIAL
15 g/½ oz fresh yeast or 1½ teaspoons dried yeast
450 ml/¾ pint warm water
1 teaspoon brown sugar
550 g/1¼ lb wholewheat flour
100 g/4 oz strong white flour
50 g/2 oz wheat germ
1 tablespoon salt
15 g/½ oz lard

Prepare the yeast liquid: blend the fresh yeast in the warm water until dissolved or dissolve the sugar in the warm water, sprinkle in the dried yeast and leave in a warm place until dissolved and frothy, about 10 minutes. Mix the wholewheat flour, white flour and wheat germ together in a large bowl. Add the salt and rub in the lard until the mixture resembles breadcrumbs. Add the yeast liquid to the dry ingredients and mix well to form a soft dough.

Turn the dough onto a lightly floured surface and knead until smooth and elastic. Place the dough inside an oiled polythene bag and leave to rise until doubled in size. Remove from the polythene bag, knock-back and knead until firm. Shape into loaves. Cover and prove.

Bake the loaves in the centre of a hot oven (230°C., 450°F., Gas Mark 8) for 25–30 minutes for a large loaf and 10 minutes for small loaves. Reduce heat to moderately hot (200°C., 400°F., Gas Mark 6) and bake for a further 15 minutes for a large and 20 minutes for small loaves.

Rich Wheat Germ Bread

Makes 3 small loaves

This is a white bread mixture with added wheat germ giving it a rich golden colour and nutty flavour.

METRIC/IMPERIAL
15 g/½ oz fresh yeast or 1½ teaspoons dried yeast
50 ml/2 fl oz warm water
1 teaspoon castor sugar
400 ml/14 fl oz warm skimmed milk
2 tablespoons vegetable oil
1 tablespoon castor sugar
2 teaspoons salt
225 g/8 oz wheat germ
550 g/1¼ lb strong white flour
cooking oil

Prepare the yeast liquid: blend the fresh yeast in the warm water until dissolved or dissolve the sugar in the warm water, sprinkle in the dried yeast and leave in a warm place until dissolved and frothy, about 10 minutes. Mix the warm skimmed milk, oil, sugar and salt together in a large bowl. Add the yeast liquid, the wheat germ and white flour and mix to form a soft dough, adding extra white flour if it is too sticky to handle.

Turn the dough out onto a lightly floured surface and knead until smooth and elastic, about 10 minutes by hand or 2–3 minutes in a mixer with a dough hook. Cover the dough and leave to rest for 10 minutes. Remove the cover and knead the dough for a further 2 minutes. Divide the dough into 3 equal pieces and shape into balls. Cover again and leave to rest for a further 10 minutes. Shape to fit three small (450-g/1-lb) well greased loaf tins. Lightly brush the tops of the loaves with cooking oil. Cover and prove for about 1½ hours in a warm place, longer in a cool one. Bake in the centre of a moderate oven (180°C., 350°F., Gas Mark 4) for 30–35 minutes. Turn out onto a wire rack and leave to cool.

Bran Plus Bread

Makes 2 small loaves

This bread is suitable for a high residue diet. It has a coarse, close texture because of the additional bran it contains, but this is offset by the nutty flavour.

METRIC/IMPERIAL
25 g/1 oz fresh yeast or 3 teaspoons dried yeast
1 tablespoon soft brown sugar
500 ml/18 fl oz warm water
675 g/1½ lb wholewheat flour
100 g/4 oz bran or Bran-Plus
1 tablespoon salt
15 g/½ oz butter or vegetable fat

Follow the directions for making, shaping and baking Wholewheat Bread (Standard Method) (see page 31), adding the bran to the flour before mixing.

Sweet Bran Bread

Makes 2 small loaves

METRIC/IMPERIAL
15 g/½ oz fresh yeast or 1½ teaspoons dried yeast
350 ml/12 fl oz warm water
2 tablespoons brown sugar
275 g/10 oz strong white flour
225 g/8 oz bran or Bran-Plus
1 tablespoon wheat germ
1 teaspoon salt
25 g/1 oz butter or margarine
1 tablespoon dark molasses or black treacle

Prepare the yeast liquid: blend the fresh yeast in the warm water until dissolved, or dissolve 1 teaspoon of the sugar in the warm water, sprinkle in the dried yeast and leave in a warm place until dissolved and frothy, for about 10 minutes. Mix the white flour, bran, wheat germ and salt together in a large bowl. Rub in the butter or margarine until the mixture resembles breadcrumbs, and then add the sugar. Stir the dark molasses or treacle into the yeast liquid and add to the dry ingredients, mixing to form a soft dough.

(At this stage it might be too sticky to handle but do not add more flour.)

Cover the dough in the bowl and leave to rise until doubled in size. Turn the dough out onto a lightly floured surface and knead for 5 minutes, adding a little extra flour if still too sticky to handle. Shape to fit two small (450-g/1-lb) well greased loaf tins. Cover and prove in a warm place for about 30 minutes. Bake in the centre of a moderate oven (180°C., 350°F., Gas Mark 4) for 30–35 minutes. Turn out onto a wire rack and cool.

Index

D

E

F

G

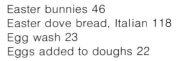